STAINED AND DECORATIVE
G·L·A·S·S

STAINED AND DECORATIVE
G·L·A·S·S

ELIZABETH MORRIS

For my parents, Tom and May Morris

A QUINTET BOOK

Published by Grange Books
An Imprint of Grange Books plc
The Grange
Grange Yard
London SE1 3AG

This edition published 1995

ISBN 1-85627-801-8

This book was designed and produced by
Quintet Publishing Limited
6 Blundell Street
London N7 9BH

ART DIRECTOR: Peter Bridgewater
DESIGNER: Linda Moore
EDITORS: Patricia Bayer, Judith Simons
PICTURE RESEARCHER: Anne-Marie Ehrlich
ILLUSTRATOR: Lorraine Harrison

Typeset in Great Britain by
Central Southern Typesetters, Eastbourne
Manufactured in Hong Kong by
Regent Publishing Services Limited
Printed in Singapore by
Star Standard Industries (Pte) Ltd

Acknowledgements

The author and publishers would like to extend
their grateful thanks to the following people, who
have advised and helped with this book: Nigel
Alder; the staff of the American Embassy Library;
American Museum, Bath; Michael Archer; Antonia
Avery; Keith Baker; Ann Barker; Rodney Bender;
Jean Burks; Hugh Carroll; Peter Cormack; Painton
Cowan; Jack Cutler; Kay Donegan; Ginger Ferrell;
Alfred Fisher; Martin Harrison; John Lawson; Tim
Lewis; Rod and Ruth Mcleod; Mary McGowan; the
staff of Time Life Library; Louie White; James
Weatherly; Alan Younger.

Picture Credits

Key: l = left; r = right; t = top; b = bottom.

The author and publishers have made every effort to identify the copyright owners of the pictures used in this publication; they apologize for any omissions and would like to thank the following:

American Red Cross: 68. Mark Angus: 118/119. © Arup Associates (Photo. Crispin Boyle): 124 b. Rodney Bender: 4/5, 72 br, 80, 81 t, 92, 95 r, 97 t, 102/103 b, 108 tl tr, 114 t, 118, 119, 120/121 b, 122. Susan Bradbury/ College of Art & Technology, Newcastle: 116/117. Richard Bryant Photography: 114 b, 120/121 t. © Ed. Carpenter (Photo. Karlis Grant): 117, 124 t. © Peter Cormack: 48/49, 49 t, 53 tl, 56 bl br, 61, 63–5, 66 r. Corning Museum of Glass, Corning. NY: 60/61. Painton Cowan: 30, 31, 34, 36–38, 53 tr b, 58, 58/59, 62/63 (V & A), 66 l, 67, 69, 72 tl tr bl, 73, 78/79, 82/83 t b, 85 b, 86–90, 95 l, 97 br. © Garth Edwards: 125 bl. E T Archive (Victoria & Albert Museum): 39, 49 b. © Glasgow Museums & Art Galleries, The Burrell Collection: 25. Courtesy of Goddard & Gibbs Studios: 15–23, 99. Martin Harrison: 42–45, 46/47, 47 t, 48, 50–51, 55, 59, 70, 70/71, 71 b, 76/77, 77, 79, 96, 100, 108 b, 112/113. Courtesy of the Haworth Art Gallery (Photo. Geoffrey Proctor): 68/69. Clive Hicks: 26, 27, 28/29 b, 32–3, 34/35. Angelo Hornak Library: 24/25, 28, 28/29 t, 30/31, 54/55, 74, 75, 104/105. Lucinda Lambton Library/Arcaid: 40/41, 52, 100/101. Courtesy of Lever Brothers Company (Photo. © Harry Wilkes): 106. Tim Lewis: 6/7, 76, 81 b, 93, 94, 98/99, 102/103 t, 106/107, 107, 109–111, 113. Gabriel Loire: 97 bl. Jacques Loire: 120, 121. © Peter Mollica (Photo. Charles Fizzell Photography): 125 tr br. Elizabeth Morris: 71 t. David O'Connor: 41, 56 t, 57. Courtesy of Pilkington Bros plc, St Helens, Lancs (Photo. Hartley Wood & Co Ltd): 7–13. © Narcissus Quagliata (Photo. Lee Fatherree): 123 (Coll. Mr & Mrs Ronald Abramson, Washington, DC), 125 tl. Alan Younger: 14/15, 47 b, 54, 84, 84/5, 85 t, 90/91, 112, 114/ 115.

CONTENTS

Chapter One: Glass   6

Chapter Two: An Art And A Craft   14

Chapter Three: From Gothic to Gothic Revival   24

Chapter Four: Victorian Revival   40

Chapter Five: The Turn Of The Century   62

Chapter Six: The Break In Ecclesiastical Tradition   78

Chapter Seven: Pubs To Palaces   98

Chapter Eight: Into The 21st Century   116

Index   126

STAINED & DECORATIVE GLASS

BY ELIZABETH MORRIS

STAINED GLASS, which can claim to be one of the oldest crafts in the world, was a major art form in Europe before painting. It has overcome – as few other arts can claim – the vicissitudes of history and fashion, in spite of living for most of its time in the shadows of architecture and painting. For long the prerogative of the Church, the image of stained glass as an almost exclusive ecclesiastic art form has remained until comparatively recently. It would also seem that its very public display has dulled the eye and any appreciation of its worth has largely been conditioned by criticism of the indifferent, rather than selection of the good. However, such prejudices are now disappearing, as a talented new international generation of stained-glass artists is creating the most exciting and vibrant work: not because they need to say something, but because they have something to say.

A number of specialist and scholarly books have dealt with particular aspects of stained glass. This book approaches the subject as an introduction, giving a brief account of both the art and the craft, primarily through American and British eyes, but noting major influences elsewhere. Time and space have limited who and what can be included, but if the consequence of this book is to create a wider interest, it will have served its purpose.

Throughout my research, I have had great support and help from those who are leaders in the field – historians, clergy, artists, authors, makers, designers, craftsmen – all of whom have generously and patiently given me their time. I am indebted to them all, and also to my family, who have encouraged my work and tolerated the disruption.

EM

JULY 1987

Chapter One

GLASS

The glass-blower cools the blob or 'gather' which he has taken from the molten glass in the furnace: Hartley Wood Glassworks, Sunderland, Tyne and Wear.

RIGHT By blowing down the hollow tube, air is used to balloon the glass into a bubble.

FAR RIGHT A 'nipple' is shaped on the end of the balloon.

IT IS DIFFICULT to imagine a home without the benefits of glass, and without the light and protection it brings. Natural glass is as old as the universe and the use of glass in building goes back to Roman times, but the art of stained glass is fairly young, having been developed over the last thousand years. Stained glass has been closely associated with history, religion, social change and scientific discovery; therein lies a fascinating story, and one that has not yet ended.

Its Discovery

THE DISCOVERY of manmade glass may have been accidental. An account by Pliny writing in the first century AD tells of travelling Phoenician merchants camping on the sandy shores of Lake Belus with their load of natron (carbonate of soda). They used natron blocks for balancing their cooking pots by the campfire and when they awoke in the morning, so the story goes, they were amazed to see that the heat of the fire had fused the natron and sand together to form glass: (sadly, this is probably an apocryphal story, as the great heat needed to form glass would have melted the cooking pots). About 3,000 years ago in Egypt, a virtually opaque glass,

made from a sand-based paste known as faïence, was used for glazes on pottery. By 1075 BC, Egyptian craftsmen had discovered the means of making almost clear glass, and at Nineveh stone tablets dating back to the 7th century BC have references to glass and glassmaking.

It was the Romans, though, who were responsible for a rapid advance in glassmaking. They mastered the production of glass, creating delicate vases and other objects, some transparent, others beautifully decorated with paint or possibly gilded. They even found a way of casting glass by pouring it onto stone, and, when cooled to a solid, using the resulting small pieces in a window. An attempt at closing an opening in a building to allow light to enter, but to exclude cold and inclement weather, is believed to have originated with the Romans (the Emperor Caligula is said to have had a form of window glass in his palace). Small, thick cast slabs mounted in wooden frames and held in place by lead strips – thought to have originated in Byzantium – were used to replace the hide, rushes or even alabaster stone previously used in countries with strong sunlight. This early albeit crude luxury has grown into today's international glass and glazing industry, with the Romans' experiments in decorating the surface of glass in continuous development ever since.

The Constituents

EARLY GLASS was made from common fine sand, whose melting point was lowered by mixing with it a flux such as wood ash. Sand is a form of silica, but quartz crystals or flint can be used as well. Soda ash is now commonly added as a flux, with limestone as a stabilizer, and often unwanted small pieces of glass, known as cullet, are included too. This mixture melts at about 2550°F/1400°C, and when annealed, or cooled, goes from its liquid state to solid glass. As the temperature is slowly dropped, the treacle-like glass can be formed by shaping it for all its many uses.

Roman glass tended to be greenish in colour because of the impurities of the iron oxides in the silica they used. Theophilus, a Benedictine monk, wrote a handbook on the crafts of the time in probably the 12th century. Called *Diversarum Artium Schedula,* or *Diverse Arts*, it described, among other things, the making of glass: 'First cut many beechwood logs and dry them out, then burn them all together in a clean place and carefully collect the ashes, taking care that you do not mix any earth or stones with them'. He detailed the building of the kilns, mixing ash with fine sand, placing a clay pot inside the kiln and then the firing until it melted, and the resulting glass when cooled.

The first recorded glassmaker in England was Laurence Vitrearius, literally, Laurence the Glassmaker. He is recorded as working in the first half of the 13th century in the south of the country, where potash produced from bracken and beechwood served to make a quite different glass from, for instance, that in southern Europe, where soda flux made from the ashes of marine plants was commonly used. The search for the right ingredients to make completely clear glass that was also strong and resisted erosion occupied the makers of glass for many centuries.

Much medieval glass was the result of trial and error, as glassmakers struggled to find the perfect ingredients and their correct proportions. Such experiments often resulted in corrosion of the surface and even gradual disintegration of some glass of this period. In the 16th century in England, Jean Carré from Antwerp was granted a 21-year licence by Elizabeth I to make window glass. In the next century, alarmed at the quantity of wood being cut to make glass and fire the furnaces, James I forbade its use by Royal Decree. The glassmakers then turned to coal as their fuel and glass manufacture moved to the north of the country, where supplies were plentiful and easily mined. Until the 19th century, window glass was taxed as a luxury in Europe and it was not until 1845 that it was finally abolished in England.

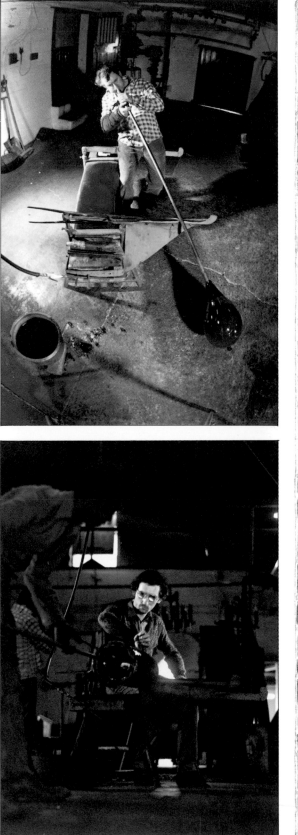

CHAPTER ONE
■

LEFT **The bubble is then swung alternately from side to side and blown again.**

BELOW LEFT **The glass is then shaped into a muff, prior to the 'disc' being removed from the end.**

RIGHT Before the glass solidifies, the ends are cut off forming a hollow cylinder.

OPPOSITE The cylinder or 'muff'.

Early Flat Glassmaking

THE VERY earliest glass manufacture entailed wrapping molten glass around a core of clay or bag of sand. When the glass cooled, the clay could be chipped away or the sand drained out of its bag, leaving a hollow-shaped vase or drinking vessel that later was given stability by adding a base on which it could stand upright. These vessels were often decorated, sometimes with colour. The first use of coloured glass was for beads and other jewellery, and also as an early form of currency. The first attempts at making flat glass by pouring molten glass onto a cooling surface resulted in a pitted and uneven sheet. Clean, clear flat glass was not produced until the method of glass-blowing was discovered.

Blowing involves the use of a hollow rod to inject air into the melt, and was probably a Syrian invention in the 2nd century BC. The glass-blower dips the rod into a pot of molten glass in the furnace, and takes out a blob known as a gather. By blowing down the tube, air is used to balloon the glass into a bubble. The bubble on the end of the blowing rod is then swung alternately from side to side and blown again, until it becomes elongated. Before the glass solidifies the ends are cut off, forming a hollow cylinder, or muff, both terms being used to describe this form of manufacture. When solid the cylinder is then cut down its length, and re-

heated for flattening and smoothing by a wood block while it is still in the 'lehr', or annealing chamber, of the kiln. The final process of cooling must be done slowly to prevent both crystallization and the shattering of the glass. This method of glassmaking is continued today, producing what is called 'antique' glass. What results is a sheet of uneven thickness and colour, giving the light coming through it great beauty and subtlety. It is this 'antique' glass that is traditionally used for stained glass. Other forms of early glassmaking included casting it and pouring it into moulds.

Colour in Glass

COLOURED GLASS was in use more than a thousand years before the discovery of how to make transparent, or white, glass. Most probably due to accidents and impurities caused in the production process, it was discovered that certain metallic oxides added to the melt resulted in coloured glass. Certainly by the 5th century AD, the Romans had found that a little copper dispersed in the melt produced a ruby-coloured glass; medieval glassmakers later discovered that the addition of manganese produced a rose-pink colour, and in the 17th century the addition of gold chloride was found to produce a beautiful, rich ruby colour. One of the first glass colours was blue, made by adding minute traces of

RIGHT The cylinder is then cut down its length ready to go into the reheating chamber (or 'lehr') where it is flattened and smoothed by a wooden block.

cobalt or copper. Green was originally the result of impurities, but later copper or iron was used.

Many of the ingredients used to produce particular colours or effects remain the manufacturer's secret even today, and the variety of hues possible is almost endless. Glass that is of a strong single colour throughout is called pot-metal glass. Streaky glass has variations of colour, while tints are pale colours. Opaque white glass was originally produced using antimony in the melt, and in 18th-century Europe it was to rival porcelain in translucency and strength. Opalescent glass, perfected in the United States towards the end of the 19th century, has a milky opaque appearance, with colours streaked through it.

Types of Glass

THE TERM 'antique' is applied to any handmade blown glass that copies medieval glassmakers' methods. This glass is full of imperfections, bubbles and surface marks called striations, and with its uneven surface and varying thickness it has a distinctive character. 'Reamy' glass is made from a mixture of white, and often coloured, glass of different hardnesses that gives it a rippled effect as the density varies. 'Seedy' glass contains myriad air bubbles, originally produced by throwing a potato into the melt to cause it to bubble and spit, trapping small amounts of air as the glass cooled.

Different blowing techniques and melts can be used to obtain different types of glass. 'Crown', or 'spun',

glass was known to have been manufactured by the Romans before the Christian era, the technique passing to France in the early 14th century. In this method the blown bubble of glass is transferred to a solid iron rod, or 'punty'. The bubble is re-heated and rotated at a high speed to create a large flat disc in which concentric circles are formed (these are made by the elongated air bubbles in the spinning glass). The flat plate, which can be up to 5 ft/1.5 m in diameter and dangerous to work with, was then cracked off the iron, leaving a 'bull's eye' of thick glass in the centre. This knob was thought to be inferior in quality to the squares that could be cut from the remainder of the disc, but is now often used to give a window a vintage look.

Other early types of glass were produced by pouring it into moulds, or, while cooling, pressing it into shapes or adding surface textures. The process known as 'flashing' involved taking clear (white) glass on the rod from the melt, blowing it into a small bubble, and then dipping the bubble into a crucible of red melt so that it carried a thin coloured coating. This process could be repeated as many as a dozen times until the desired density of red, or other colour, was achieved. The coloured 'flash' could later be selectively ground away until the clear white glass was revealed, thus enabling two colours to appear on a single piece of glass. After the medieval glassmakers' success in making red flashing, blue and green were also introduced, and all were often used in the 16th century and later for heraldic stained glass.

New Production Methods

AS FLAT GLASS became more widely used for general window glazing, so new methods of production were invented to meet the growing demand. Two methods revolutionized glassmaking at the beginning of the 19th century: the first, drawing a ribbon of glass vertically from the melt, letting it cool as it travelled away from the furnace and then cutting it up into sheets, and, secondly, rolling glass by passing it in a treacly state through two rollers to flatten it into a ribbon. The later refinement of polishing the surface of the glass produced the smooth clarity of plate glass. Rolling and drawing also provided the means of making a cheap and plentiful supply of coloured glass to meet the growing demand for stained glass. Referred to as 'cathedral' glass, it lacks the character and beauty of 'antique' glass (when a second colour is included, it is known as 'streaky cathedral'). The use of rollers also allowed pattern and texture to be pressed onto the glass in its manufacture and, although most commonly found in clear glass, patterned coloured glass is also made – sometimes to try and imitate the striations on the surface of 'antique' glass.

In the 19th century, box-shaped moulds were introduced in which molten glass was blown against the sides, and, when solidified, cut up into rectangles. These slabs of glass were thick in the centre and tapered to a thinner edge, giving great depth of colour and beauty. It was developed in 1889 by E S Prior and, because of its resemblance to 13th-century glass, it was known as Prior's Early English. Chance Brothers made a similar glass that they termed Norman.

Modern Glass

THE INVENTION in England of the float-glass process in the 1950s has now made all other methods of producing clear flat glass obsolete. In this technique the liquid glass is floated on a bed of molten tin, producing almost perfectly smooth parallel sides to give great clarity – and allow cheap mass-production.

New techniques in decorative drawn or rolled glass include coating its surface with hot glue to produce surface fractures, adding small particles or chips of different colours to the cooling surface in manufacture, and creating by other methods ever more varied surface effects, such as the increasingly popular American rippled 'water' glass. Fusing one glass with another is a growing area of interest, and can allow many contrasting colours in a single piece of glass. More and more, it seems the only limitation on the type of glass that can be produced is the glassmaker's imagination.

AN ART AND A CRAFT

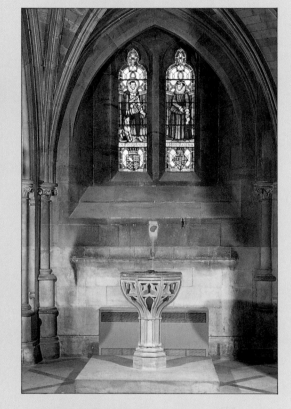

Stained glass designed by John Lawson and executed by
Goddard and Gibbs Studios. The Cathedral of Our Lady
and St Philip Howard, Arundel, Sussex.

RIGHT A completed design for a stained-glass window, illustrated to scale.

CENTRE RIGHT The initial design is usually executed in watercolour, since its transparency is most suited to depicting the translucence of glass.

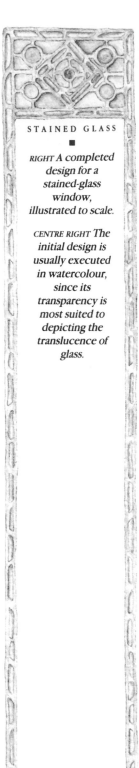

· St Philip Howard ·

& Anne Dacre his wife

THE MAKING OF a stained-glass window has changed little in a thousand years, and the materials and tools are for the most part developments of those used by medieval glaziers. Until recently, the craft had been almost exclusively the province of the professional because, unlike, for example, the woodworker, the glazier's materials were comparatively scarce and expensive. However, spurred by the recent enthusiasm for crafts and by a growing number of glass shops and mail-order companies, stained glass is now a major amateur hobby – with many practical books available on the subject. Coupled with this has been a growing appreciation and interest in the history of art generally, which has in turn helped make stained glass popular. The following brief description of the various stages in the making of a window, and also the principal techniques used in decorating glass, give an indication of the different, demanding skills involved.

Design

THE DEVELOPMENT of an idea for a window requires both a practical knowledge of glass, including how it can be used and supported, and an aesthetic understanding of colour and light, and how these two are affected by such things as aspect and environment. The subject of the window, its size and height, and the limitations imposed by its surroundings are, among other things, all important to the stained-glass artist. Normally the design is executed in watercolour to indicate something of the translucence of glass: more elaborate designs might involve models and samples. The purpose is to illustrate to scale what the finished window will look like.

CARTOON

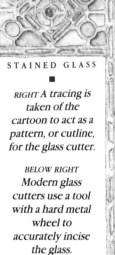

Cartoon

THE CARTOON is a full-size working drawing taken from the design. It shows the exact dimensions of the completed window, defining the areas and shapes of lead and glass, and illustrates all the painted work. The early glaziers made their full-scale drawings for the window on a flat white table, after accurately measuring the aperture to be filled. Later, cartoons executed on paper became works of art in their own right – instead of merely a means to an end – and some Victorian examples included the use of colour.

Cutline

THIS IS a tracing taken from the cartoon, which acts as a pattern for each piece of glass. Two methods are commonly employed: either a single tracing on which the glass cutter lays his sheet of glass and cuts just inside the outline of the shape so as to allow for the thickness of the lead framing strip, or the method wherein individual paper templates for each piece of glass are made by cutting out each shape using double-bladed scissors, again to allow for the thickness of the lead strip. The former is popular in the United States and Great Britain, the latter in France and Germany. The same patterns are used by the lead worker in assembling the window.

■

LEFT The cut sections of glass are temporarily mounted onto a sheet of glass with wax or plasticine.

RIGHT Paint is applied to the glass with a broad-bristled brush, used exclusively for shading, or 'matting'.

Glass Cutting

IN MEDIEVAL times, the glass cutter used a red-hot iron or rod to break the glass. Around the 16th century, the pointed diamond was introduced to score the glass, with the resulting surface fracture then over-stressed by tapping or pressure to give a clean-edged break. Nowadays a cutter with a hard metal wheel is widely used, which allows very accurate and complex shapes to be cut. Files, grinders or special 'grozing' pliers are used to break or chip off any unwanted edges. After the glass shape has been cut, it is then temporarily placed on a large glass plate with wax or plasticine, so that the cutter can build up the window without lead, ensuring that the colour, tonal value and type of glass all faithfully follow the design. Once the glass has been selected and cut, the basis of the window is settled.

Aciding

ACID CAN BE used to produce two different colours on a single piece of flashed glass – where a darker colour is always laid on a lighter colour or white, and then selectively removed by acid to reveal the base colour. The principle of the process is simple: the areas of glass that are not to be acided are protected by a resist such as beeswax or bitumen and the whole is then immersed in a bath of dilute acid that eats away at the unprotected glass. The length of time it remains in the bath depends on the depth of colour to be removed, with some colours taking longer than others to be eroded. However, the practice can be dangerous because of the involvement of acid, and requires great care. Before the discovery of hydrofluoric acid in the last century, the flash of glass was rubbed away, or abraded, using flint or powdered stone. Aciding can produce an infinite variety of tones without affecting translucency, and is of particular benefit in heraldic work.

Painting

IN PREPARATION for painting, the cut pieces of glass, still temporarily fixed to their glass plate, are placed in front of a window or over a back-illuminated, glass-topped table. The only pigment used is a black or brown vitreous paint, consisting of powdered glass with iron or copper oxide, a flux usually of gum arabic, and a thinner. The paint is applied to the inside of the glass with special brushes: broad bristled for shading, known as 'matting', and a thinner brush for 'line' work, for painting details such as faces and folds in clothing. A bristle brush can be used for a stippled effect, and glass painters have many other variations to suit their own

particular skills. Much use is made of scratching out as well. The object of this form of painting is to control or exclude the light coming through the glass. Enamel painting is different, employing metal oxide-based paints to transmit their colour.

Staining

YELLOW 'STAIN', discovered at the beginning of the 14th century or earlier, gives stained glass its generic name. A silver-nitrate solution, with added agents for adhesion and thinning, is applied to the surface of the glass with a brush, and then fired at a moderate temperature in a kiln. The result is a yellow stain on the glass, ranging from the palest lemon to orange, depending on the constituents of the stain solution. It can also be used to produce, among other hues, the colour green on blue glass.

Firing

IN ORDER to fuse the paint, or stain, and the glass permanently together, they must be fired in a kiln. The glass, with the paint work uppermost on its surface, is laid on a tray with a perfectly flat bed (to prevent distortion when it cools) and placed in the kiln. The temperature is raised to between 1100° and 1300°F (600° and 700°C), at which time the glass begins to become soft, thus allowing the paint to sink into its surface. As the temperature is slowly lowered to prevent stresses remaining in the glass as it cools, the paint fuses to the glass. Usually stain is fired into the glass at a lower temperature, after the paint firing.

BELOW LEFT A finer brush is used to detail areas such as the face or hands of a figure, a process known as 'line' work.

*ABOVE AND RIGHT
After firing, the
pieces of glass are
framed with lead
strips, called
cames.*

*OPPOSITE ABOVE The
inside of a window
in Canterbury
Cathedral showing
medieval
feramenta, using
iron pegs to secure
the stained glass.*

*OPPOSITE BELOW The
'cement' mixture is
forced under the
cames with a stiff
brush to seal the
panels of glass.*

Leading

ON COMPLETION of the firing process, the pieces of glass are ready for framing. Lead is the traditional and still most widely used means of framing the glass shapes: it has strength yet limited elasticity when the glass is moved by temperature or wind pressure, it is very malleable and can be easily bent to almost any shape, and it also has good durability due to its initial corrosion forming a protective surface.

The lead strips are manufactured to form an 'H' section to allow the glass to be inserted in each edge, and are called cames, after the medieval practice of pouring molten lead into boxes of reeds (or 'calms') to make it into thin strips for glazing work. Later the cames were cast in wood or iron moulds, and in the 16th century the lead mill was invented. Where there is a join in the lead cames, caused by either an alteration in direction or change of lead profile, a soldered joint is made on each side.

Sealing

THIS PROCESS is often referred to as 'cementing' and involves a mix of items such as boiled linseed oil, red lead, turpentine and lamp black which are added to a base made of plaster of Paris and powdered whitening. This mixture is forced under the leaves of the cames by a stiff bristled brush, and the surplus removed by soaking it up with sawdust or powdered whiting – all before the panel is finally cleaned. The sealing prevents the ingress of wind-driven rainwater, and also gives the panel limited rigidity.

Copperfoil

AT THE END of the 19th century, a new method of framing pieces of glass was developed in the United States by Louis C Tiffany, involving slender copper tape that he wrapped around the edge of each piece of glass. When the glass was placed against its adjacent piece, the join had a string of solder laid along its length, resulting in a neat and permanent connection. This method allowed very small pieces of glass to be framed and joined together, thus overcoming the difficulty of achieving sharply curved designs. The best examples of this method are Tiffany's stained-glass lampshades.

Installation

FIXING THE stained glass into its opening requires a strong frame and permanent seal at the edges. Originally the frames – normally of stone or wood – would be the openings themselves, and the glass would be inserted into a groove or held in a rebate by the use of a 'bead' (in stonework, a thin fillet of cement at the edges), or with a wood frame and separate strip of wood. It is now common to fix the glass into a separate metal sub-frame, often of painted aluminium, and to set this into the opening. To help prevent the glass panels from sagging under their own weight or bending from wind pressure, bars are placed across the opening; copper wires that have been soldered to the lead cames are then twisted around them, thereby attaching the glass to the bars. The horizontal bars across a panel are called saddle bars, and, when placed where two panels are joined by an overlapping came, are known as division bars. A system of heavy vertical and horizontal bars used both for support and security is termed 'feramenta'. Support bars were once made of iron but, because of the damage corrosive iron can cause to stonework, are now normally of a non-ferrous metal such as bronze. Many modern windows have a continuous metal strip following the line of the lead came across the panel, giving added strength and support.

Engraving

THE SURFACE decoration of flat glass by means of working into the material itself – as opposed to laying on paint or stain – is traditionally achieved by engraving, embossing or sandblasting. Engraving involves cutting into the surface of the glass and, since the middle of the 16th century, has been done using a diamond point. It became very popular in Italy, spreading first to the Tyrol and then to the Netherlands and England in the 17th and 18th centuries. A form of engraving known as 'brilliant cutting' originated in the United States, and arrived in England c 1850. In this abrasive process, the design is cut into the surface of the glass using a large, rapidly revolving stone wheel, following which the rough edges on the glass are smoothed by a wooden wheel and then polished with a revolving brush.

Embossing

GLASS WHOSE surface has been eroded by acid is termed embossed. Different acids and different strengths produce degrees of obscuration and surface textures. These effects can be used singly or in a combination to produce a design on the surface of the glass. A further refinement is the addition of paint, or even precious metals such as gold leaf, which is laid on or rubbed into the acided surface. Although acids were known earlier, embossing itself dates from the 19th century and the discovery of hydrofluoric acid.

Sandblasting

THIS METHOD of abrading glass has been in use since about 1880 and is carried out by bombarding the glass surface with a stream of particles. The idea originated from observing windows in seaside buildings that were scratched and dulled by the impact of sand blown against them. As in acid-etching, the area to be protected is covered by a resistant layer of a material such as rubber or lead, and the exposed area of glass is then eroded to the required depth. The result can vary from slight obscuration of the surface to a deep moulded relief that imparts a sculptural form to the glass.

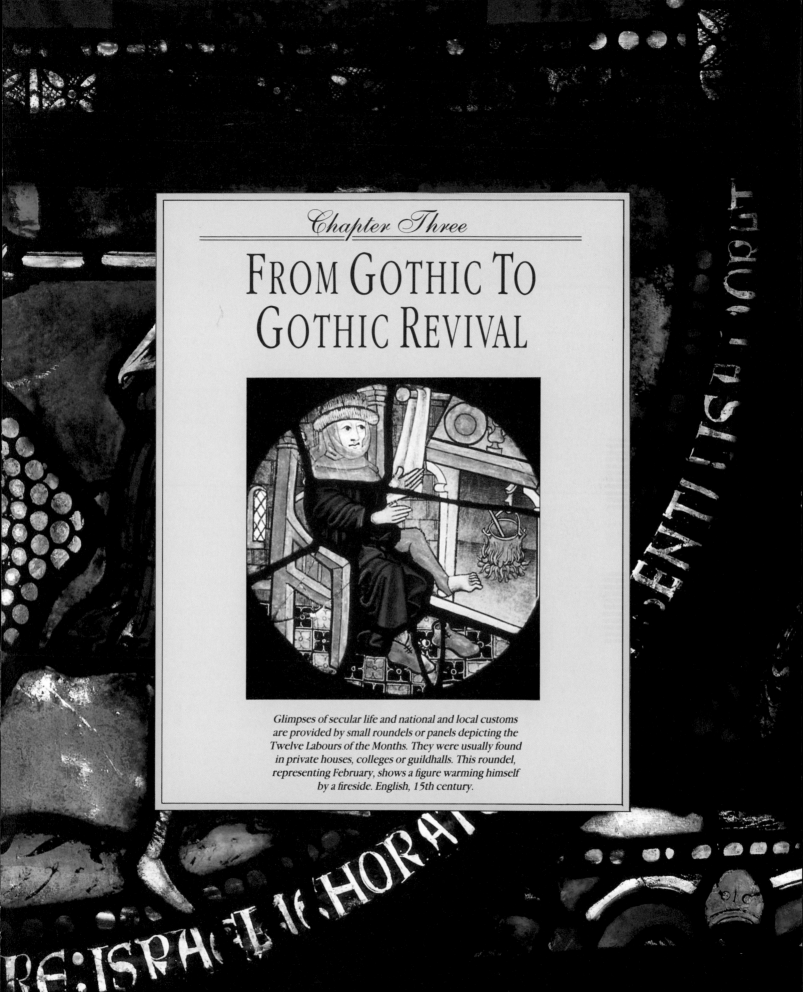

FROM GOTHIC TO GOTHIC REVIVAL

Glimpses of secular life and national and local customs are provided by small roundels or panels depicting the Twelve Labours of the Months. They were usually found in private houses, colleges or guildhalls. This roundel, representing February, shows a figure warming himself by a fireside. English, 15th century.

THE OLDEST GLASS IN ENGLAND C·1150

THERE CAN BE FEW people who are not moved as they stand beneath a medieval stained-glass window, gazing at the glowing colours and intricate pattern, perhaps set in a delicate web of stone tracery. Sunlight streaming through lays at their feet the medieval glazier's art, which has survived nearly a millennium of war, plague and iconoclasm. Stained glass is as much a part of Gothic architecture as soaring vaulted naves and lavishly carved porches.

The oldest surviving stained-glass windows are preserved in Augsburg Cathedral in Germany, and are thought to date from the end of the 11th century. They depict five monumental Romanesque-style Old Testament figures gazing sternly across the nave. Attributed to the monks at Tergensee, they display a technique resembling that of the 6th- and 7th-century Byzantine mosaics at Ravenna, Italy. It was, however, a development in architecture, rather than art, that nurtured the flowering of medieval stained glass.

Gothic Architecture

THE PERIOD of architecture known as Gothic – a derogatory 18th-century reference to the barbaric Goths – had its birth in the 12th century, when Abbé Suger began to rebuild the rich and powerful royal abbey of St Denis in Paris. By this time the graceful pointed arch had begun to replace the squat round arch of Romanesque architecture. Previously only small isolated windows could pierce the walls and thick pillars that supported the weight of the roof. But at St Denis much of the thrust of the roof vault was carried to the ground independently of the walls by outside buttresses, allowing between them 'wonderful and uninterrupted light of the most radiant windows'. As luxury and daring were expressed in increasing height, so the buttress projected further out, thus becoming the 'flying' buttress – the symbol of Gothic architecture.

The Gothic style admirably expressed growing affluence, the power of the Church and the genuine religious zeal of the time. Magnificent cathedrals soared above town roofs, displaying rich carvings and stained glass. Probably the most beautiful as well as the best preserved early Gothic cathedral is at Chartres in France, which was begun at the end of the 12th century after fire had destroyed an earlier church on the site. Its scale, architectural confidence and window glazing influenced building and stained glass throughout Europe from the 13th century onward. The windows remain an inspiration and wonder to the onlooker today, as well as a testament to the skill of the craftsmen who created them.

LEFT The north rose window in Chartres Cathedral, known as the Rose of France, was donated by Blanche of Castile, the mother of Louis IX. The window incorporates lilies, the emblem of Louis, and the arms of Blanche can be seen in the lancets below.

■

RIGHT The Five Sisters window in York Minster is the finest and largest example of 'grisaille' to be found in England. The window is an intricate cobweb of foliage and ornamental patterns.

Early English Stained Glass

IT IS DIFFICULT to identify the first purely English stained glass. Only a small amount of clear glass was being made at this time, and any coloured glass was imported from the Continent. In 1174, the choir of Canterbury Cathedral was destroyed by fire and, as a result of close Anglo-Norman links at the time, a Norman, William of Sens, was invited to England to help restore the cathedral. He brought with him both stone for rebuilding and coloured glass for the windows. The earliest stained glass in Canterbury appears in the north rose window, which seems to have been completed by 1178. However, an earlier example, thought to date from 1150, can be found at York Minster, in a single remaining panel depicting a king seated in the branches of a Jesse Tree. Gradually the building of great English cathedrals and enlargement of important Saxon churches began to compete with the magnificence of the monastic abbeys, which until then had reigned supreme. Rich stained glass often filled the windows as each building sought to impress its neighbours and worshippers, even in the humblest parish churches.

It was, however, sometimes a matter of controversy whether the so-called 'rainbow of light' should or should not fill a church. Ascetics like Bernard of Clairvaux, founder of the strict Cistercian Order, disapproved of these 'coloured gems' and declared that too much ornament in a church distracted men's minds and diverted monks from contemplation. In 1134, the Chapter of the order decreed that only clear glass could be used in the windows of their churches. Following this edict to live 'pure and harmonious lives', a grey/green-tinted glass with simple geometric and natural patterns, known as 'grisaille', was introduced. Because it was cheaper than coloured glass, it became widely used. A fine example of this work is the Five Sisters window in York Minster, and there is another in the Lady Chapel window at Hereford Cathedral.

Pictures in Glass

THROUGHOUT THE medieval period, the Church wielded great power over the community. Simple untutored men and women received religious instruction – and sometimes thinly veiled propaganda – through stories depicted in stained glass. Knowledge, formerly available only in frescoes, mosaics and sculpture, was now imparted through the pictures in the windows. The images were symbolic, not factual; for example, the 12th-century window in Canterbury Cathedral called *Adam Delving* represents the Garden of Eden as a single etiolated tree.

CHAPTER THREE
■

LEFT Quarries – small square- or diamond-shaped panels – often depict birds or animals. This one, from the Zouche Chapel in York Minster, shows a bird stalking a spider.

BELOW LEFT Detail of a miracle window, known as the Jordan Window. It tells the story of the family of Sir Jordan Fitzeifulf on a pilgrimage to Thomas à Becket's tomb at Canterbury to seek miracle cures. Trinity Chapel, Canterbury Cathedral, c 1220.

The stories in the windows were based on events and characters from the Old Testament known as 'types', and paralleled those characters and events thought to reappear in the New Testament that were termed 'ante-types'. For example, Jonah being swallowed by the whale and delivered up after three days prefigures Christ's Entombment and Resurrection. A good series of these windows is at King's College Chapel, Cambridge. The genealogy of Christ was a popular subject, as were stories from *The Golden Legend*, a book that related the lives and legends of the saints. There was no attempt to present the figures realistically, a practice that mirrored the visual art of the period in tapestry, heraldry and frescoes.

Windows depicting lives and miracles of the saints were used for intercession – and woe betide anyone who, having received a benefit from one of these saints, failed to give the Church gifts in money or kind in payment. Such saints would be placed in the windows in a stained-glass framework or canopy to show their importance. Initially the canopies were simple, but as time passed they followed the architectural style and became very tall and grand. The borders were often made up in grisaille and decorated with lozenges, circles or squares in a geometric pattern, or foliage, and, particularly in the 14th century, with tiny heraldic devices, faces or **grotesques**. Stained glass was expensive and small remaining pieces would be used up in this way to eliminate waste. By the 16th century, the use of a wide border design around the window had dwindled or even disappeared. The figures themselves spread across the design and the canopies were depicted as alcoves with supporting pillars that soared up into pinnacles and occasionally occupied half the window.

Symbolic or iconographic imagery was gathered from the Bible, in those days the Latin Vulgate version. Perhaps the most famous symbol was the Jesse Tree. It represents in picture form the prophecy of Isaiah that the Messiah would descend from Jesse, the father of King David. This royal lineage was depicted by a tree growing from Jesse's loin with Mary as its stem and Christ as its fruit or flower. The earliest example of this iconography can be seen at St Denis, but the finest Jesse Tree is generally held to be that in the west wall at Chartres. An interesting example at Dorchester Abbey in Oxfordshire, has the stone tracery of the window as the tree and the stained-glass panels as the branches.

Simple portraits of the donor of the window or part of the building first appeared in the representation of Abbé Suger in an apse window in St Denis. Figures would normally be depicted at the foot of the window, sometimes with wives and children kneeling in supplication or holding out a model of the church or window to the saint to whom it was dedicated.

Occasionally the figures appeared in tracery lights and their heraldry was shown in the form of simple shields, indicating the name and rank of the donor so that their benevolence might be recognized. Details of costume indicated the status of a donor figure – a king wore a crown, a bishop a mitre. Subsequently, as Eastern influence filtered in via the Crusades and later through trade, the style of dress altered to reflect the times.

CHAPTER THREE

■

LEFT Adam Delving *is one of a series of windows in the choir clerestory of Canterbury Cathedral depicting the ancestry of Christ.*

BELOW LEFT Ornate *14th-century canopy in Gedney Church, Lincolnshire. The window depicts architectural features and is surrounded by a border of stylized foliage.*

STAINED GLASS

■

RIGHT **This window
in the Abbey
Church of St Denis
in Paris depicts the
kneeling figure of
Abbé Suger, who
had the church
rebuilt in 1140.**

Mid-Gothic

BY THE BEGINNING of the 14th century, it is estimated that some 80 cathedrals and 500 churches of near-cathedral size had been started in France alone, following the consecration of St Denis. In England the early Gothic cathedrals of Lincoln, Wells and Salisbury were built at this time. Later the style called 'Opus Francigenum' – in recognition of its origin – inspired the builders of the great cathedrals of Cologne and Strasbourg in Germany, Siena in Italy (with its marbled striped façade), and those at Búrgos, Toledo and León in Spain.

As the plague known as the Black Death took its toll, the 14th century saw the population of England reduced by one-third. By this time the Early English Period of architecture had given way to the mid-Gothic Decorated Period. Sadly, much 13th-century glass was removed or broken to make way for the new, freer style, with its tracery and curved shapes. Windows often became larger and the areas of glass between the stone mullions longer and narrower, with tracery above. Small pictures were created across the lights, and stylized design gave way to more flowing forms.

Painting and Staining

DURING THIS period, as the glaziers vied with each other to create ever more beautiful windows, painting, using oxides of iron fired into the glass, became more naturalistic. The discovery of staining in the early 14th century gave glaziers a completely new palette of yellows – as well as the name of their craft. This technique involved the application of a nitrate of silver to white glass which, when fired in a kiln, stained the glass yellow. The glass painters were enthusiastic in their use of this new 'colour' and introduced it at every possible opportunity. It is thought that one of the windows in the north aisle of the nave of York Minster contains the first use of this technique in English glass painting. One of its advantages was that larger pieces of glass could be used, resulting in fewer lead lines; for instance, a head could also include a crown and halo.

Another technique dating from Romanesque times was the flashing of glass. This involved taking a base of white glass onto which was added a thin layer or 'flash' of red glass. This could be abraded away in places, allowing white and red on the same piece of glass. Ruby was the most common colour in this treatment – in some areas the ruby flash could be left, and in others removed to leave the clear glass underneath, which could then be yellow stained and painted. By the 16th century blue glass was also treated in this way, allowing heraldic devices to be accurately portrayed in stained-glass windows.

LEFT *This Jesse Tree is believed to be one of the first windows of its kind and the model for many others. It shows the genealogy of Christ and dates from c 1140. Notre Dame Cathedral, Chartres.*

THE ROSE WINDOW

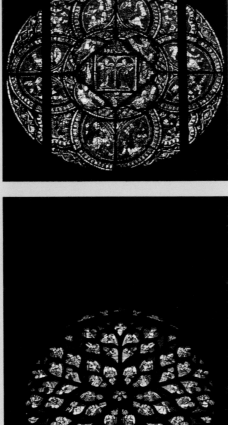

PERHAPS THE most significant French contribution to the European fervour of building was the introduction and development of the great round window. The earlier type of crude Romanesque wheel window now gradually blossomed into the rose window, that complex and intricate geometrical pattern of slender stone and glorious coloured light. Suspended between heaven and earth at the west end, and sometimes also in the north or south transept wall, the rose window depicted eternity and infinity in perfect symmetry and order, with Christ as its centre. Earlier windows were usually placed in the façade, perhaps filling the pointed arch form completely, as at Reims Cathedral. With the development of Gothic architecture, the rose window became more magnificent and important, sometimes forming part of a wall of minimal and delicate tracery, such as at Notre Dame in Paris. Later the tracery patterns within the rose itself became more flamboyant, and nowhere is this better seen than at Sens Cathedral in France. However, by the mid-16th century one of the most beautiful inspirations of Gothic architecture had faded completely.

TOP England's only surviving 12th-century rose window, showing The Law and the Prophets. The central circle dates from 1178 and depicts Moses and a blindfolded figure, symbolizing the Synagogue, holding the symbols of law, surrounded by four women representing the virtues. North rose window, Canterbury Cathedral.

ABOVE The rose window in Sens Cathedral typifies the flamboyant tracery patterns of 16th-century Gothic architecture.

RIGHT The rose window above the west door of Reims Cathedral is a glorious example of 13th-century bar tracery.

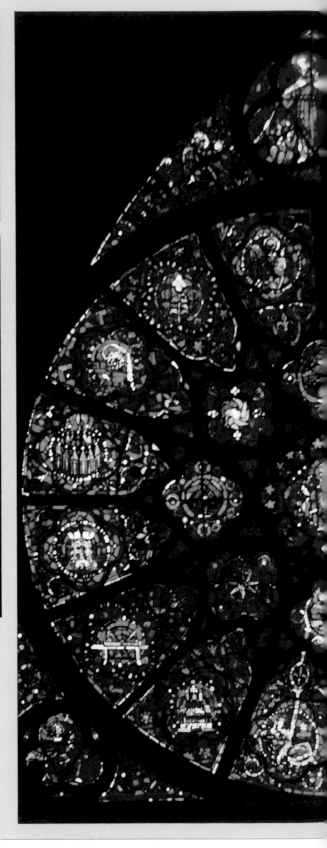

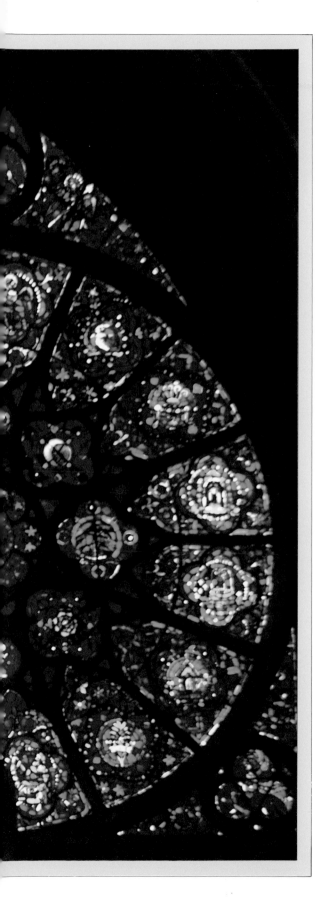

Late Gothic

THE 15TH CENTURY was a time of growing prosperity, despite the War of the Roses in England and fighting that racked the Continent. Stained glass was part of a flourishing artistic endeavour that spread across Europe. In England rich wool and cloth merchants, anxious to secure a place in the afterlife, gave freely towards the cost of windows and the building of bigger churches. Coloured glass, however, was still expensive, even for well-to-do merchants, and as windows in the new Perpendicular style became larger, they incorporated more clear glass with increased painting and staining.

Merchants' marks on windows depicting tools or symbols connected with their trade – as well as windows donated by the crafts guilds themselves – give an interesting insight into the ordinary domestic lives of both rich and poor in the Middle Ages. Roundels showing the Twelve Labours of the Months, already popular in northern Europe, were placed in private houses, colleges, guildhalls and occasionally churches.

Rise of the Renaissance

SCHOOLS OF skilled glass painters emerged at Norwich and York, both with distinctive styles and especially adept at figure painting. Elsewhere, new talent and innovation also appeared. At Warwick John Prudde, the King's Glazier, included in his stained-glass decoration holes drilled in the hems of garments of distinguished figures in which he placed small pieces of coloured glass, creating the effect of jewels. It is interesting that Theophilus, probably writing in the 12th century, had described coloured glass being ground into powder to make a paste, which when fired onto the glass was used as 'jewels' to decorate crowns or mitres: this process, however, proved unsatisfactory, as the 'jewels' fell off. Later attempts in the 15th century to stick coloured glass onto clear panes to achieve a similar effect were equally unsuccessful.

By the end of the 1400s, the invention of the printing press had meant that woodcuts were widely available. This had a very powerful influence on stained glass, as ready-made popular designs, including the works of masters such as Holbein and Dürer, could be reproduced by the painter on stained glass without the involvement of an artist. Painting became much more subtle in colour and shading, and a new flesh tone was achieved by the application of sanguine. The use of enamel paints became increasingly common in the search for realism, and leading – which in earlier work had helped to create a picture with a strong outline –

■

RIGHT To create the decorative border on the male figure's gown, the glazier made holes into which small pieces of coloured glass were inserted. Lady Chapel, Evreux, France.

now became less important. Some of the finest painted glass was in the form of small roundels of genre and landscape scenes, at which Flemish and Swiss artists in particular excelled.

Sadly, the influence of the Renaissance masters had a detrimental effect as the glaziers tried to copy the meticulous details of the painting, thus ignoring the lead lines and making a picture *on* glass instead of a picture *from* glass. The result was uninspired and heavy, with the glass losing its sparkle and translucency. By the end of the 15th century, the skills that had been acquired over 300 years began to fade.

The Reformation

THE PROTESTANT revolutions in northern Europe in the early 16th century resulted in enormous upheaval, with many people fleeing their homes and even their countries. German and Flemish glaziers emigrated to England and set up workshops at Southwark, where their arrival was bitterly resented by the English glass painters who had practised there since the 13th century. The emigrants' finest work appears in King's College Chapel at Cambridge, which is a watershed in the art of English stained glass. This climax of Renaissance stained glass, commissioned in 1515 and not finished until about 1540, depicts events of the Christian faith, from the Annunciation to the Assumption. To achieve this monumental task, the glaziers adopted a new method, carrying the picture right across the window lights and intervening stone mullions, as though painting a huge canvas. However one may admire the artistic quality of the painted glass, the role of the glazier had been totally subordinated to that of the painter. With the increasing use of paint and, later, enamels, pot-metal glass fell from favour and became scarce. This in turn encouraged more enamel painting, and beautiful mouth-blown coloured glass in windows all but disappeared.

The dissolution of the monasteries by Henry VIII, from 1536 to 1540, caused the destruction of many religious works of art, none suffering as much as stained glass. Whole windows were broken up, and more: in the Lady Chapel in Ely Cathedral, all the beautiful carvings, as well as the glass, were smashed wantonly. The result of this ruination was the loss of much of the country's medieval glass.

LEFT This window, painted by the van Linge brothers, shows St John the Evangelist and St John the Baptist with the arms of the St John Tregoze family in the foliage of a tree. Lydiard Tregoze, Wiltshire, c 1630.

BELOW LEFT Christ Redeems Souls from Hell, *one of 26 windows in the main chapel of King's College, Cambridge, dating from 1515 to 1530.*

STAINED GLASS

■

RIGHT 28 late-15th-century windows remain intact in St Mary's Church, Fairford, Gloucestershire. This panel depicts the Mouth of Hell from the Last Judgement window.

BELOW RIGHT Enamel-painted 18th-century window depicting the Baptism in the River Jordan, designed by Francisco Slater and painted by Joshua Price. Church of St Michael and All Angels, Great Witley, Worcestershre.

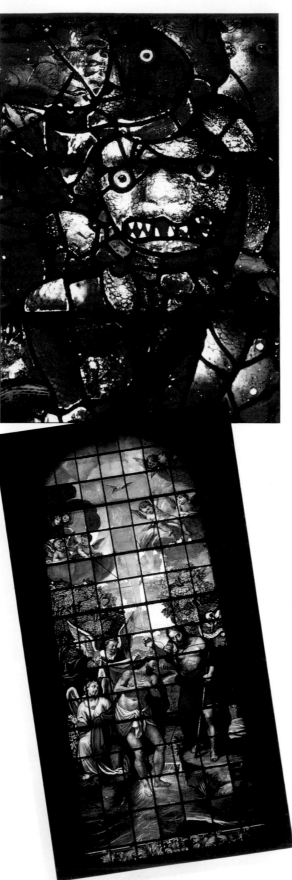

17th-Century Enamel Painting

IT WAS NOT until the destruction in the previous century had abated that a religious revival in the early 1600s allowed the use of stained glass again. Skills, however, had been largely lost, including that of making coloured glass. Enamelling by painting coloured pigment directly onto the surface of clear glass together with staining became common, with rectangular panes being used to fill a window.

Under the patronage of Archbishop William Laud, two exceptional Flemish enamel painters, the brothers Abraham and Bernard van Linge, were invited to England, where they executed a number of richly coloured pictorial and figurative windows. The best of these may be seen in the Oxford colleges of Balliol, Christ Church, Wadham and Lincoln, and also in the east window of Peterhouse College, Cambridge, and at Lydiard Tregoze in Wiltshire. Similar work by Baptista Sutton, an Englishman who was well known during this period, can be seen at the Trinity Chapel of the Abbot's Hospital in Guildford. The increase in stained-glass work at this time was such that the London Glaziers' Guild petitioned successfully to become a City Company.

The revival, however, was short-lived. Following the executions of Charles I and Archbishop Laud, the Cromwellian era brought forth a new outbreak of iconoclasm – and the loss of more glass. In some instances, only crucifixes and faces were vandalized, but there were also instances where the glass was removed and hidden for safety, or even, as at York, preserved in exchange for surrender of the city. One exceptional example that survived was the series of 28 magnificent 15th-century windows at St Mary's Church in Fairford, Gloucestershire. It was not until after the Restoration of 1660 that religious tolerance returned.

In the latter half of the century, with stained-glass skills at a low ebb, heraldic painting came to the fore. Heraldic devices had been used on the Continent as early as the 13th century and appear in stained glass at Chartres; the earliest surviving English examples are in the west window of Salisbury Cathedral. By the end of the 17th century, the leading painter was Henry Gyles of York (1645–1709), whose work was meticulous in detail and extremely elaborate: examples are in University College, Oxford, and Acomb, North Yorkshire, where Charles II's coat of arms may be seen. In North America the Dutchman Everett Duycking, who settled in New Amsterdam – now New York – in the mid-17th century, was paid in furs for his heraldic painting on glass.

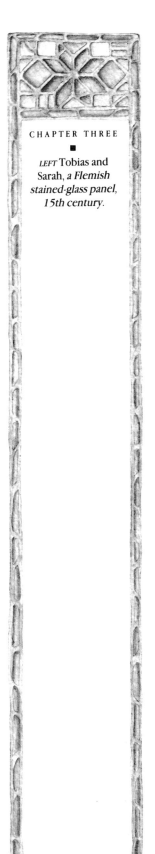

LEFT Tobias and Sarah, *a Flemish stained-glass panel, 15th century.*

The 18th Century

DURING THE 1700s, the Price family carried on this tradition of heraldic work in England. The brothers William and Joshua and the latter's son, William, followed the techniques initiated by the van Linges. It is thought that Joshua was the most gifted of the family, and his enamel painting on a series of windows in Great Witley Church, in Worcestershire, is a fine example of his work. The west window of Westminster Abbey was painted by William Price the Younger in 1735; other examples by the family are the rose window in the north transept of Westminster Abbey and fine windows on the south side of New College Chapel, Oxford.

Toward the end of the century there was little interest in stained glass, and what remained often suffered from lack of repair and unsympathetic restoration. However, connoisseurs such as William Jerningham and Horace Walpole began to study and collect antiquities, including stained glass (though others, like James Wyatt, regarded it as 'barbaric'). This flicker of interest was to become a flame of extraordinary brightness in the next century. Meanwhile, across the channel in France, the Revolution was destroying a wealth of medieval and later glass, though Chartres Cathedral was to be spared the destruction.

…rauitque nomen eius moyses dicens quia
…aqua tuli eum

…aaron loquetur pro t…
…cmm tu autem eris ei in…

IAO

Chapter Four

VICTORIAN REVIVAL

Detail of The Flight into Egypt, designed by Edward
Burne-Jones for Morris & Co, 1862. St Michael's Church,
Brighton, E Sussex.

OVERLEAF Window by Morris & Co, 1870. Holy Trinity Church, Meole Brace, Shropshire.

RIGHT Window depicting the Apostles in St Mary's College Chapel (RC), Oscott, Sutton Coldfield, Warwickshire. Designed by Augustus Pugin and executed by William Warrington in 1838.

CENTRE RIGHT This window, designed by J H Powell in 1869 for John Hardman & Co, shows Jonathan and his armour-bearer. St Dunstan's Church, Cheam, Surrey.

THE 19TH CENTURY spanned an era of immense social, political and industrial change, both in Europe and North America. Architecture and art reflected the aspirations, technical innovation and growing wealth of the industrial nations. Style and fashion too, spread by improving communications, increasingly influenced the arts and for the first time allowed a national and later an international market. To satisfy demand, industry and art turned to each other, passing from almost total independence at the beginning of the century to fashion-conscious interdependence at the end. Stained glass was no exception in this industrial and artistic revolution.

The previous century's use of colour on, rather than in, glass continued in the early years. Stained glass was the skill of the painter, filling his glass canvas with a picture that ignored glazing bars and used the building structure as its frame. What now displaced this was a return to the skill of the medieval craftsman and the rediscovery of the beauty of glass itself. It was this going back to the fundamentals of stained glass that enabled the revival of the early part of the century to blossom into a thriving craft industry, eventually employing hundreds of workers.

Gothic Revival

THE ORIGINS of this reappraisal lay in the previous century, when a study of history and archaeology, and an appreciation of the arts, became fashionable. Grand Tours to the Continent by the wealthy produced an interest in classical art and medieval history and the collections of art resulting from these tours were displayed, discussed and written about. Thus, what had started as a hobby became an influence – and grew into a style. Foremost among these great collectors was Horace Walpole (1717–97), son of the great Whig Prime Minister of England, whose house outside London, called Strawberry Hill, exemplified the Gothic Revival. Among Walpole's vast art collection were examples of painted Flemish and other glass, which excited the interest of many of his visitors. These included the leaders and creators of fashion of the time, such as the architect Augustus Welby Pugin (1812–52).

Pugin was the son of a French architect who had fled to England to escape the French Revolution in 1798. He followed his father's profession and later became the foremost architect of his day in England, taking a leading role in establishing the Gothic Revival both in theory and in practice, with a devotional approach spurred on by his conversion to Roman Catholicism at the age of 21. His first church, St Mary's in Derby, coincided with Victoria's accession to the throne in 1837, and a fruitful partnership with Sir Charles Barry resulted in his work in the rebuilding of the Houses of Parliament. He successfully developed the early principles of stained glass in spirit as well as design, making much use of it in his own home in Ramsgate. Pugin was a perfectionist, however, and was unable to find a glass painter whom he believed had the necessary sympathy to interpret his designs. He eventually turned to John Hardman, whose studio was to grow into one of the biggest in the country, remaining in family ownership until 1959.

LEFT *Designed by Augustus Pugin and made by William Warrington in 1838, this window depicts the Virgin and Child. St Mary's College chapel (RC), Oscott, Sutton Coldfield, Warwickshire.*

RIGHT Christ in Glory by Michael O'Connor, 1871, reveals the designer's distinctive geometric style in the canopies. St Andrew's Church, Trent, Dorset.

FAR RIGHT
Window by Thomas Willement in Winchester College, 1854.

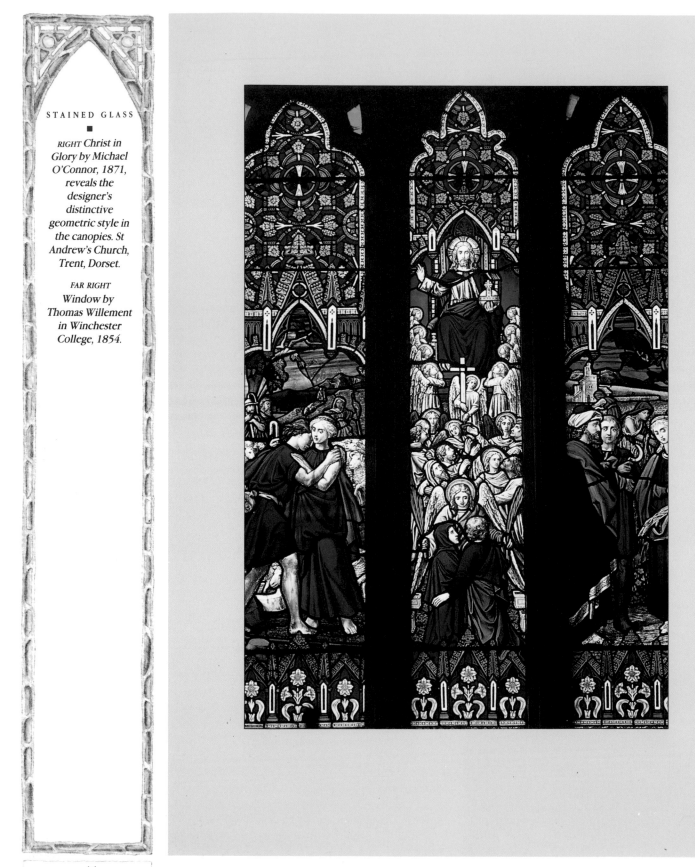

STAINED GLASS

■

RIGHT AND FAR RIGHT
The Flight into
Egypt by William
Wailes, 1864, in All
Saints Church,
Boyne Hill,
Berkshire.

The First Half of the Century

THE FOREMOST English stained-glass designer in the early part of the century was Thomas Willement, who was later to have the grand title of Heraldic Artist to King George IV and Artist in Stained Glass to Queen Victoria. He pioneered the breakaway from the contemporary picture-painting school of glass artists, taking his inspiration from the medieval glaziers. The work carried out by the Shropshire firm of Betton & Evans on the windows of Winchester College provided him with useful knowledge of early stained glass. He made his first window in 1812, and although initially his work was fairly crude, he soon developed a style reminiscent of medieval glass. A typical Willement window contained vignettes of biblical scenes surrounded by borders of foliage or geometric designs. Some of his finest work was in heraldic stained glass, of which the best known is probably the great memorial window at Hampton Court. Two of Willement's pupils, William Warrington and Michael O'Connor, both worked in the new Gothic Revival style, and carried out several commissions from Pugin's designs in his churches. Pugin also employed William Wailes of Newcastle to make some of his windows.

The man who made one of the greatest contributions to the revival of stained glass was neither a stained-glass artist nor a craftsman. There had been several unsuccessful experiments seeking to manufacture glass similar to the strongly coloured glass used by medieval glaziers. In the late 1840s Charles Winston, barrister, antiquarian and connoisseur, determined to rediscover the secrets of making pot-metal glass, having been inspired at the age of 18 to design and execute a stained-glass window for his father's church at Faringham. Helped by a Dr Medlock of the Royal College of Chemistry, he discovered that, for instance, the main constituent of blue glass was cobalt – not lapis lazuli as had been previously thought. Similarly, other pieces of early glass were analysed with the help of chemists employed by the firm of James Powell of Whitefriars.

Around this time, William Edward Chance, a Birmingham glass manufacturer, was also experimenting; eventually, after many years of devoted work, he succeeded in producing glass of a superior quality. As a result of these successful experiments, it again became possible to make the best pot-metal glass (known as 'antique' because of its medieval origins), with much of it produced by James Powell & Sons at their Whitefriars Glass Works and Chance Brothers at Smethwick.

BELOW LEFT Thomas Willement often incorporated fragments of 13th-century glass in his own work. His sign (his initials superimposed) can be seen above the inscription. Creech Church, near Wareham, Dorset.

THIS·CHAPEL·WAS·FITTED·VP·AT·THE·EXPENSE·O
JOHN·BOND·OF·GRANGE·ESQ:AS·A·CHAPEL·OF·EAS
TO·THE·PARISH·OF·STEEPLE·A·D·1840·HE·SVRVIVED·T

THE GROWTH OF STAINED-GLASS STUDIOS

BY THE MIDDLE of the century, with the support of the influential Cambridge Camden Society and the rise of Anglo-Catholicism, the Victorian imagination was fired and the Gothic style dominated architecture and stained glass in England. This new-found enthusiasm, combined with evangelical fervour in religion, resulted in an enormous surge in the number of churches being built, as well as the 'Gothicization' of existing ones. This latter practice was spurred on by the Camden Society, which wanted to rid churches of differing architectural styles. In the second half of the century, Victorian ecclesiastical stained glass moved on from its origins in Gothic Revivalism, and developed into a style of its own. This followed the pictorial tradition of early years, but was increasingly expressed in bold, strongly coloured designs, with confidently painted large-scale biblical figures and scenes. Of course, styles varied and fashions changed, and with work rarely signed, or even recorded, the more than 80,000 stained-glass windows produced during Victoria's reign can be a bewildering maze for anyone but the expert.

However, some studios rose

OPPOSITE LEFT The Dawning of the Last Day, *by Frederick Ashwin, 1871, is the only recorded work by this stained-glass artist in Britain. He emigrated to Sydney and founded one of Australia's first stained-glass studios. St Barnabas' Church, Hengoed, Shropshire.*

ABOVE Two early windows by N H J Westlake for Lavers & Barraud, 1864. St John the Baptist, Cookham Dean, Berkshire.

ABOVE RIGHT The east rose window in Waltham Abbey, Essex, is an early work by Edward Burne-Jones for James Powell & Sons, 1861.

RIGHT Queen Victoria Golden Jubilee window by Heaton Butler & Bayne, 1887. Great Barton Church, Suffolk.

above the rest in quality and sheer artistry. Among them were Clayton & Bell, which became one of the largest; Heaton Butler & Bayne; Lavers Barraud & Westlake, and later, in the 1870s, Burlison & Grylls. The Gibbs family and Henry Holiday, many of whose early designs were carried out by the famous firm of James Powell & Sons, also had well-known studios. Their work enriched the Victorian churches of England, the makers usually going un-recognized – except perhaps for the rare symbol or even rarer name – and they remain today a delight to be discovered and enjoyed.

RIGHT St George and the Dragon, by C Edwin Gwilt for Niton House, Isle of Wight, 1840. Now in the Victoria & Albert Museum, London.

Clayton & Bell

THE PARTNERSHIP of J R Clayton and Alfred Bell was formed while they were both working in the large architectural practice of Gilbert Scott. There they also formed a friendship with the architects G F Bodley and G E Street, who were later to give them important commissions. Their first windows, designed together, were for the nave clerestory in Westminster Abbey and were probably made by the London studio of either Lavers & Barraud or Ward & Hughes. Later they teamed up for a few years with Heaton & Butler, who executed their designs (afterwards the latter were joined by Robert Bayne, probably a pupil of Clayton & Bell, to form their own company). One of their most successful commissions, for the church of St Mary the Virgin at Hanley Castle, Worcestershire, was given to them by Street in 1860. The west window of the Last Judgement is an outstanding example of Clayton & Bell's artistic skill in design and use of colour, and is among the best stained glass produced in this period.

Commissions were soon flooding in, and Clayton & Bell moved to large new premises in London's Regent Street, where they eventually employed about 300 people in their studio. They became one of the most successful stained-glass studios in the second half of the century and carried out commissions for the Queen – for which they received the Royal Warrant. Their work can be found all over England, gracing great cathedrals as well as small parish churches. Two of their most notable accomplishments were the large west window of King's College Chapel, Cambridge, and the east window of Bath Abbey. Their work is also in the United States, and includes the window of St Paul Preaching on Mars Hill, in New York's Church of the Incarnation on Madison Avenue and 35th Street. Almost inevitably the freshness and vitality of Clayton & Bell's earlier work suffered from the enormous output demanded of them, and their later windows can be heavy and stereotyped. By the time of Bell's death in 1895, the firm was being run by their sons. Michael Farrar-Bell, Alfred Bell's descendant, continues his family's tradition to this day.

BELOW RIGHT **The Expulsion of Adam and Eve, by Charles Eamer Kempe, 1890. St George's Church, W Grinstead, Sussex.**

Charles Eamer Kempe

ANOTHER LARGE and famous studio that carried the medieval tradition of stained glass into the 20th century was that of a gifted and deeply religious man, Charles Eamer Kempe. He was born the fifth son of wealthy parents (who gave their name to the Kemp Town development in Brighton), and his main ambition when at Pembroke College, Oxford, was to become a clergyman. This aim was thwarted by a serious speech defect, however, leaving him to pursue his great talent in church decoration and stained glass. He studied under the great neo-Gothic architect G F Bodley and later became a pupil with the firm of Clayton & Bell.

As a child, Kempe was supposed to have had a mystical experience in Gloucester Cathedral, induced by the setting sun casting its light through the windows, and this was said to have strengthened his resolve to work with stained glass in later life. His earliest recorded window, in fact, is Gloucester Cathedral's Bishop Hooper Memorial Window, made by Clayton & Bell in 1865. By 1866 Kempe had set up as an independent designer with two assistants, in a studio that he opened at his London home. Already considered an authority on medieval stained glass, Kempe was consulted on the restoration of the ancient glass at Fairford Church near Cirencester and Nettlestead Church in Kent.

15th-century stained glass was to inspire Kempe's style and influence all his ecclesiastical stained-glass work. His use of blue, green and ruby glass and large areas of silver staining, combined with the delicate and detailed painting of the figures, was a hallmark of his style. His popularity grew, and by the end of the century he was employing more than 50 people. He completed 3,141 commissions for stained glass in Britain and abroad, particularly in the United States, where his glass may be seen in New Haven, Connecticut, in Philadelphia and in the National Cathedral in Washington, DC. One of his largest and most successful commissions in England was for Winchester Cathedral.

In spite of a certain amount of repetition of early designs in his later work, occasioned by great success and demand, Kempe never allowed the quality or individuality of his work to deteriorate. His work can often be recognized by the characteristic soft colouring, the exacting draughtsmanship, the angels' wings 'coloured like peacock feathers', and, after 1895, by the use of a wheatsheaf symbol – taken from his family arms – to sign his work. At the end of the century, when other artists were taking up a new, freer style, Kempe remained loyal to the classic Victorian tradition, which the firm carried on even after his sudden death in London in 1907. He bequeathed the company to his cousin Walter Ernest Tower who, together with four of Kempe's previous colleagues, continued it as a limited company, signing their work with a tower incorporated in the wheatsheaf symbol. His most famous pupil was Ninian Comper and he, with others, continued Kempe's traditional approach to stained glass, even after the Second World War.

■

FAR LEFT Window designed by C E Kempe for Thomas Baillie & Co, 1868. St Mark's Church, Stapleford, Sussex.

LEFT AND BELOW LEFT This early four-light window by C E Kempe shows the use of silver stain to great effect, 1876. St John the Evangelist, High Cross, Hertfordshire.

53

The Pre-Raphaelites

STAINED GLASS

■

BELOW RIGHT
*Window designed
by Dante Gabriel
Rossetti for Morris
& Co, 1862, and
adapted from a
design for the east
window in
Bradford
Cathedral.
Manningham
Church, Bradford,
Yorkshire.*

THE PRE-RAPHAELITE Brotherhood, founded in 1848 by, among others, William Holman Hunt, John Everett Millais and Dante Gabriel Rossetti, was an important painterly adjunct to the Gothic Revival. Employing new colouring and bold flowing line to emphasize and enhance designs, they rejected what they considered to be the illusionary idealism of Raphael. The art critic John Ruskin declared, 'Pre-Raphaelitism has but one principle, that of uncompromising truth in all that it does, obtained by working everything down to the most minute detail from nature only' – a belief that truth was to be found in scrupulous attention to fact.

The growing influence of this group affected both art and stained glass as well as the critics and, in turn, the public. However, the man who dominated not only stained glass but all the applied arts through the latter half of the century – and beyond – was William Morris.

William Morris

WILLIAM MORRIS'S influence in the arts and crafts of the second half of the century is almost incalculable. He was, like Kempe, the son of wealthy parents; after leaving Oxford University, where he began his friendship with Edward Burne-Jones, he was able to indulge his belief in the importance of the individual's contribution in an age of growing mass-production. His workshop was founded in 1861 and set up as a craftsmen's co-operative, advocating a return to the high standards of the past in craft and design.

Joined by Burne-Jones, Rossetti, Ford Madox Brown, Philip Webb, Charles Faulkner and P P Marshall, Morris started the firm of Morris, Marshall, Faulkner & Company, the only money in hand being £1 from each partner, a contribution from Morris's mother and a further small amount of cash from each of them. Their aim was to achieve beauty in all things, declaring 'the aim of art is to increase the happiness of men . . .', and they became a close-knit band of artists. Some of their work was displayed at London's second great International Exhibition of 1862 and, with growing publicity and recognition, they prospered, eventually moving to larger premises with more staff, including apprentices recruited from the boys' home in Euston Road, London.

In contrast to other stained-glass work at that time, they adopted a free-flowing style in both lead lines and painting with strong vibrant colours and naturalistic form. Burne-Jones was the artist who put the firm's ideas into designs and cartoons: one of his most successful windows is that of the Kingdom of Heaven in St Michael and All Angels, Lyndhurst, Hampshire, 1862–63. As well as ecclesiastical work, they carried out many domestic commissions, some as part of their wide-ranging decorative skills that encompassed textile and wallpaper production, furniture making and printing.

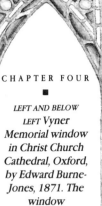

CHAPTER FOUR
■

LEFT AND BELOW LEFT Vyner Memorial window in Christ Church Cathedral, Oxford, by Edward Burne-Jones, 1871. *The window commemorates the death of four undergraduates in Greece.*

RIGHT AND FAR RIGHT *Two panels depicting The Flight into Egypt by Edward Burne-Jones for Morris & Co, 1862. St Michael's Church, Brighton, E Sussex.*

BELOW RIGHT *Detail of a window depicting Adam and Noah by Ford Madox Brown for Morris & Co, 1865. All Saints Church, Middleton Cheney, Northamptonshire.*

BELOW FAR RIGHT *St Matthew window by Morris & Co, 1862. Lady Chapel, Christchurch, Southgate, London.*

And I heard the number of them which wer

Adam   Noah

The book of the generation of Jesus Christ

LEFT Two windows depicting the Baptism of Christ by Edward Burne-Jones for Morris & Co, 1862. St Michael's Church, Brighton, E Sussex.

RIGHT **The Angel Musician** *by Edward Burne-Jones for Morris & Co, 1882, is very rich in colour and punctuated with decorative stars. St Peter and St Paul, Cattistock, Dorset.*

CENTRE RIGHT **Window by Morris & Co in Holy Trinity Church, Sloane Street, London, 1873.**

The Aesthetic Movement

MORRIS'S IDEALS were taken up by others, who, while perhaps not sharing his socialist principles, reacted against High Victorian taste in the traditional treatment of stained glass. They believed in a decorative art in harmony with the surrounding architecture, taking its inspiration from nature and natural form. Their figures were full of movement and grace, with backgrounds of leaves and plants. Stained glass in hall windows, borders to doors, and fanlights became fashionable, and opened up new markets. The standard of work was generally high and the designs original, although even Burne-Jones could often only meet demand by adapting previously successful work – his figure of St Martin, designed for the east window of St Martin, Brampton, Cumberland, in 1880, was thought to have been repeated at least 40 times between 1883 and 1935.

One of the most significant stained-glass artists at this

LEFT Window
designed by Henry
Holiday for Lavers
& Barraud, 1865,
in Worcester
College, Oxford.

time was Henry Holiday. He rejected sheer imitation of the Gothic style and instead took his inspiration from Classical and Renaissance art. Much of his work was executed by James Powell & Sons, although in 1891 he set up his own workshop. His circle included Harry Ellis Wooldridge and Carl Almquist, a Swede who later became chief designer for the Lancaster firm of Shrigley & Hunt. They and their followers of the years 1870 to 1885 are included among the adherents of the so-called Aesthetic Movement, and their stained glass is generally recognizable by its use of muted colour and classical figures. Good examples of their work are Holiday's windows of 1869 in St Mary Magdalene, Paddington, and Wooldridge's chancel windows at All Saints, West Bromwich, Staffordshire, executed in 1873.

In Scotland and the north of England, the work of the stained-glass artist Daniel Cottier became extremely popular. In 1873, he opened studios in New York and Sydney, thus spreading the contemporary style of English stained glass and finding a close affinity with Tiffany and La Farge.

STAINED GLASS

■

RIGHT Window produced by Tiffany Studios at their Corona glassworks on Long Island, entitled Reading of the Scrolls.

Southern Germany and France

KING LUDWIG I of Bavaria, an eccentric patron of the arts, founded the Munich workshop of·the Royal Bavarian Glass Painting Studio in 1827. It was at the centre of the 19th-century revival of stained glass in Germany, and, largely influenced by Italian art, produced predominantly biblical work of indifferent quality. The workshop's heavily enamelled glass, rich and ebullient in the Baroque and Rococo styles, was exported to the United States and some European countries including Scotland, where its windows for Glasgow Cathedral, although in the 19th-century Gothic style, were widely deprecated. The studio continued, however, to enjoy considerable success and appreciation in Germany, where much of its stained glass was lost in the two world wars.

In the 1840s there was a growing popularity for a group of young German painters who worked in a deserted monastery in Rome and became known as the Nazarenes. They copied such masters as Raphael, Dürer and Perugino, and their 'brotherhood' relationship anticipated the English Pre-Raphaelites. Prints of their work were popular with stained-glass artists and remained fashionable in Germany until the end of the century

In France, Eugène-Emanuel Viollet-le-Duc believed, like many of his contemporaries, that colour in glass should replace the duller enamel painting then fashionable. As the Inspector of the Service des Monuments Historiques under Napoleon III, he was responsible for the maintenance and restoration of stained-glass windows throughout France, and was therefore in an excellent position not only to influence style in stained glass, but also to do something about his belief. He allied himself with the so-called 'Scientific Romantics', who were pledged to revive stained glass in its pure early Gothic form; as a result of their activities, much restoration of old glass was carried out and many new workshops opened. Work came from all over Europe, and when in the 1850s the Roman Catholic Archdiocese of New York began building a new cathedral, the commission for the stained glass was given to Henry Ely of Nantes and Nicholas Lorin of Chartres.

Another Frenchman, Eugène Stanislas Oudinot, also carried out commissions for American churches; his window, *The Supper at Emmaus,* is in Christ Episcopal Church in the Bronx. Although the Gothic Revival was slow to be embraced in France, with many people still favouring enamelling in the neo-classical or Baroque style, the stained glass at the Paris Exposition Univer-

selle of 1855 encouraged its development and led to wide acceptance of its use, particularly in secular buildings. By the end of the century, stained glass in the new Art Nouveau style was appearing in shops, cafés and office buildings.

Early American Stained Glass

THE FEW GLAZIERS among the very early American colonists had neither the materials nor the skills for making stained-glass windows, and it is unlikely that anyone could have afforded to commission them. The very few immigrants who were stained-glass artists, most of them from England, brought with them the traditions and fashions of Europe: only later was there a truly American school of stained glass. The great turning point was the introduction of opalescent glass in 1880, when American ideas began to flow to Europe.

One of the earliest names in American stained-glass work is that of Richard Upjohn, who was the architect of and, it is believed, designed the windows for, Trinity Church, at Broadway and Wall Street, Manhattan (1844–

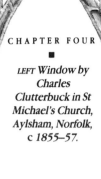

CHAPTER FOUR

■

LEFT Window by
Charles
Clutterbuck in St
Michael's Church,
Aylsham, Norfolk,
c 1855–57.

45). However, very little indigenous stained glass was produced until after the middle of the century, when William Jay Bolton, son of a wealthy family who emigrated to the United States from England in 1836, came to the fore. His first stained-glass window was for his family church in Pelham Bay in New York State's Westchester County, which was followed by numerous commissions, including 60 windows for the Church of St Ann and the Holy Trinity in Brooklyn Heights, New York. These, along with the windows at Trinity Church, are thought to be the earliest surviving stained-glass windows in the country in situ. The oldest stained-glass studio is the firm of J & R Lamb, founded in New York City in 1857 by the English-educated Joseph Lamb, who was assisted by his brother Richard; the firm's tradition is now carried on by Lamb's grandson, Frederick.

Opalescent Glass

IN 1865, a young American artist named Louis Comfort Tiffany crossed the Atlantic to Europe. In France he became fascinated by the richly coloured medieval windows in Chartres Cathedral, and when he compared these with the new stained glass being produced at that time, he found much of the modern glass dull and lifeless, the more so when it was heavily painted. Back in New York in the early 1870s, he began to experiment, seeking to re-create the quality of medieval glass. He noted in a letter that 'I perceived that glass used for claret bottles and preserve jars was richer, finer and had a more beautiful quality than any glass I could buy. So I set to puzzling out this curious matter and found that the glass from which bottles are made contained the oxides of iron and other impurities which are left in the sand when melted.'

In 1878, Tiffany founded his own glass works, but after a fire continued his experiments at the Heide Glasshouse in Brooklyn, where he found John La Farge carrying out similar work. Together they produced a new glass, which they called 'Favrile', from the Latin for fabricated. Favrile glass was streaked with hues of its own and other colours; the colour was strong and the variety endless, often iridescent and of a milky, opalescent appearance. This opalescent glass became the hallmark of Tiffany's stained glass, and quickly spread in popularity from America to Europe.

Chapter Five

THE TURN OF THE CENTURY

AD·MAJORE M·DEI·GLORIAM
ET·IN·PIAM MEMORIAM
CAROLI·BAKER·TEESDALE

*Detail of the east window in Lamarsh Church, Essex, by
Mary Lowndes, 1896.*

STAINED GLASS

■

OVERLEAF Window by Dante Gabriel Rossetti depicting the wedding feast of St George and his bride. Now in the Victoria & Albert Museum, London.

RIGHT The Annunciation, c 1898, by Louis Davis, an influential stained-glass artist in Scotland as well as in England. St Mary's Church, Kelvedon, Essex.

THE ARTS AND CRAFTS MOVEMENT arose from the celebrated art critic John Ruskin's enthusiasm for crafts and craftsman – the creative workman unhindered by uniformity or mass-production and striving for both utility in purpose and beauty in design. The artist/craftsman was the ideal, implementing or at least supervising the work throughout each stage, promoting individualism and rejecting the encroachment of mass-production in manufacture. Ruskin's ideals, taken up and so passionately expressed by Morris and his followers, were the intellectual beginnings of a movement that encompassed not only stained glass but other crafts such as textiles, pottery, furniture making and printing. The Century Guild, formed in 1882 by A H Mackmurdo, was, although short-lived, one of the earliest guilds of the Arts and Crafts Movement. Two years later, in March 1884, the Art Workers' Guild was founded by pupils of the famous architect Richard Norman Shaw, who saw their work as art more than a professional process bound by convention and formality. Their motto was 'the unity of the arts', and they welcomed fellow-thinking artists and craftsmen.

The first Arts and Crafts Exhibition, held in London in 1888, proved a great success and subsequent exhibitions followed. By the 1890s, enthusiasm for the movement was apparent in the many small workshops – some grandly calling themselves 'Guilds' – that catered for the growing demand for Arts and Crafts products in the home, and as architectural decoration. The art colleges took up the new fashion as well, and their teaching served to influence a new generation. In the United States and Europe, similar ideals and movements sprang up as a result of their national social reactions to mass-production. The Arts and Crafts ideal reached its peak in the early years of this century and it was not until the Second World War that it finally lost its appeal.

Of the two main styles of Arts and Crafts stained glass, one was the striking 'new' look achieved by the use of slab glass and unusual, often abstract, designs using brilliant colour; the other was the more pictorial and traditional stained glass much in demand, known as 'Kempe' style (after Charles Eamer Kempe), which continued to be popular in England and the United States until the 1930s. Typical of the Arts and Crafts style was the use of more lifelike figures in the windows, in marked contrast to the stiff Victorian forms. Several of the artists could be identified by certain characteristics, for example, Louis Davis always designed beautiful angelic figures in swirling drapery with jewel-like colours and sinuous lead lines, while Selwyn Image's work could be identified by his distinctive style of leading.

Prior's Early English Slab Glass

THE ARTS AND Crafts studios also sought to use only the finest glass, so that in 1888 when a new type of glass was developed that combined bright colour with subtle beauty, they quickly recognized its revolutionary effect. This glass, known as 'Prior's Early English' and made in Southwark by Britten & Gilson, was a thick, heavy and unevenly textured blown glass, quite unlike the thinner sheets of 'antique' glass. It was made by blowing the molten glass into a box-shaped mould; when cold, the glass was turned out and cut into four rectangular slabs that were thicker at the centre than around the edges, thereby creating denser colour in the middle. With this new glass, lead lines became an important part of the composition. Likewise, the use of intense, vibrant colours, such as purples, blues, 'gold-pink' and emerald, became a hallmark of Arts and Crafts stained glass. A high percentage of white glass was also used; it had a streaky appearance that, combined with matted painting, toned down the intensity of the light and enhanced the iridescent colouring within the glass itself.

LEFT This detail of a five-light window, Christopher Whall's first commission, depicts St Michael and Eve, 1890–91 Lady Chapel, St Mary's Church, Stamford, Lincolnshire.

RIGHT An Arts and Crafts three-light window by Mary Lowndes and Isabel Gloag, 1901. St Mary's Church, Slough, Buckinghamshire.

FAR RIGHT Detail of a window by Mary Lowndes, 1910, in Lamarsh Church, Essex.

Christopher Whall and His Circle

CHRISTOPHER WHALL, who led the Arts and Crafts Movement in stained glass, initially took up painting. He found his career as an artist unsuccessful, however, and in the 1880s turned to making stained glass. Eventually he set up as an independent designer, greatly influencing his contemporary craftsmen who were reacting against High Victorian taste.

Mary Lowndes, a follower of Whall and one of the earliest female stained-glass artists, took the opportunity of collaborating with the Southwark glass manufacturing firm of Britten & Gilson, which offered stained-glass artists the opportunity to work on their own commissions on their factory premises. With Alfred Drury, another gifted artist/craftsman, she founded the firm of Lowndes & Drury. In 1906, they moved to The Glass House at Lettice Street in Fulham, London; this became a popular 'open house studio', where artists could work in a fully staffed stained-glass workshop,

supervising every stage of their work – a process very much in line with the ideals of the Arts and Crafts Movement. Mary Lowndes herself made at least 100 windows, occasionally working with other artists, such as Isabel Gloag.

In Ireland in 1903, another woman stained-glass artist, Sarah Purser, founded a similar workshop in Dublin, An Túr Gloine (the Tower of Glass), with Alfred Child, a pupil of Whall's, as manager. These studios were central to the development of stained glass in Ireland and were to employ such talented artists as Evie Hone, Harry Clarke, Wilhelmina Geddes and Michael Healy. The women took an equal place with the men in the creation of stained-glass windows, and equally sought opportunities within the Arts and Crafts Movement for the exchange of ideas with the same idealistic goal – that of harnessing and manipulating light to beautify and enhance their creations.

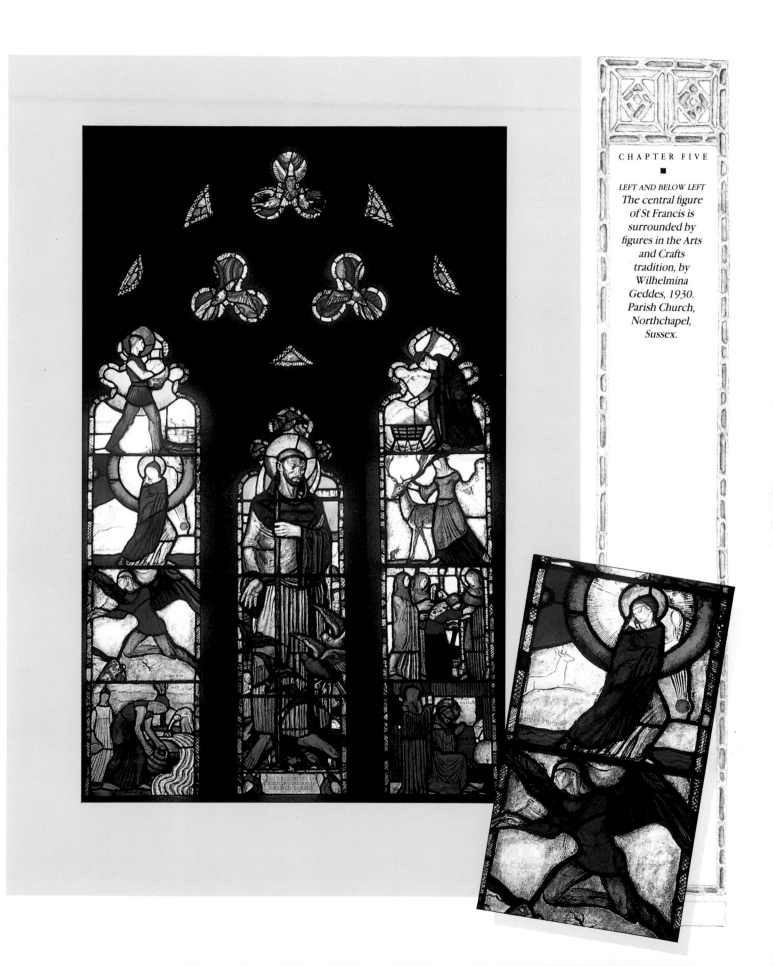

LEFT AND BELOW LEFT
The central figure of St Francis is surrounded by figures in the Arts and Crafts tradition, by Wilhelmina Geddes, 1930. Parish Church, Northchapel, Sussex.

TIFFANY

WHILE THE Arts and Crafts Movement in England and Europe was influencing new stained glass there, the work of Louis Comfort Tiffany had begun to excite the fashionable and influential in the United States, where his father's shop in New York was already well known for its jewellery and silverware designs. Using his own opalescent glass, and working with his friend Samuel Colman, Tiffany's first company – called Louis C Tiffany and Associated Artists – undertook a number of important commissions in New York, including the Seventh Regiment Armory on Park Avenue and the Union League Club (now demolished) on Fifth Avenue and 39th Street. In conjunction with John La Farge, with whom he was later to quarrel, he decorated his own house on East 26th Street. Tiffany's stained glass caused a sensation, and soon he was winning commissions to decorate the houses of the rich and famous. The height of his own success came with a commission from President Chester A Arthur to decorate the White House; much of his opalescent glass was used, including a large screen of brightly coloured panels featuring national emblems (later, sadly, the screen was destroyed).

In 1885, he renamed his business the Tiffany Glass Company, and his style became fashionable all over the country. His fame spread to Europe as well, and in France he found an admirer and friend in Samuel Bing. Bing was an important supporter of a new movement in the arts in Paris called the Nabis. Like the Arts and Crafts Movement in Britain, the Nabis' ideals spread and they began to influence art and decoration. The first result of collaboration between Tiffany and Bing was a window called *The Four Seasons,* exhibited in Paris in 1892 and later in London. This work, with its strong and separated colours, its use of small jewel-like pieces of glass, and its free-flowing design, was pure decoration and delighted all those seeking to find a 'new art'.

BELOW Tiffany stained-glass window, one of three designed for the Red Cross headquarters in Washington, DC.

RIGHT Cockatoo window produced by Tiffany Studios and now in the Haworth Art Gallery, Accrington, Lancashire.

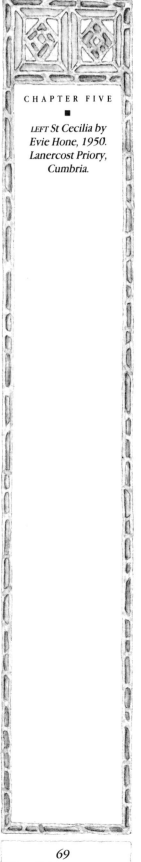

*LEFT St Cecilia by
Evie Hone, 1950.
Lanercost Priory,
Cumbria.*

STAINED GLASS

■

RIGHT The
Adoration of the
Magi by Harry
Clarke. Ashdown
Park, Sussex.

CENTRE RIGHT
Window designed
by Selwyn Image,
1881, for a private
house in
Mortehoe, Devon.

LEFT Window by
Charles Eamer
Kempe. His
traditional pictorial
designs inspired
the 'Kempe' style
popular at the turn
of the century.

BELOW LEFT
Window
produced by
George Hedgeland
from a design by
Frank Howard,
1853. St Matthew's
Church, Ipswich,
Suffolk.

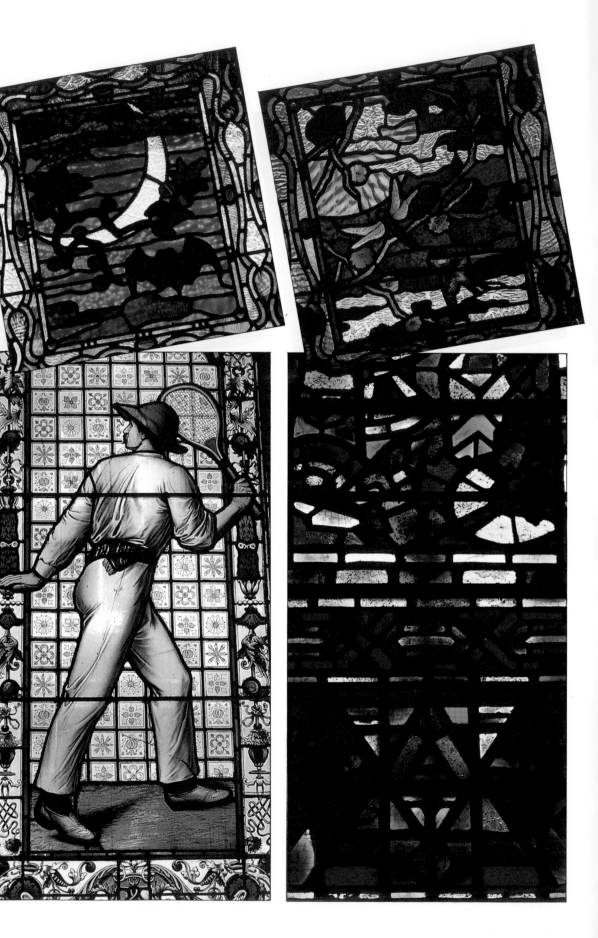

RIGHT AND FAR RIGHT
Two beautiful
Japanese-inspired
Art Nouveau
panels by William
Stewart, c 1888.
Colearne House,
Auchterarder,
Scotland.

BELOW RIGHT Tennis
Player, one of eight
panels depicting
sportsmen in the
Café Royal Oyster
Bar, Edinburgh, by
Ballantine and
designed by Tom
Wilson, 1890s.

BELOW FAR RIGHT
Detail of the west
window in St
Mary's Church,
Slough,
Buckinghamshire,
designed by Alfred
Wolmark, 1915.
Wolmark was one
of the first stained-
glass artists to use
abstract designs in
his work.

OPPOSITE Boer War
memorial window
by Louis C Tiffany,
1900. The water
bottle at David's
side is made from
the 'bull' or eye of
a piece of crown-
yellow glass. St
Cuthbert's Church,
Edinburgh.

Art Nouveau

IN 1895, BING opened a shop in Paris, calling it *La Maison de l'Art Nouveau*. Among the many furnishings and decorative objects sold in the shop was stained glass, including Tiffany's distinctive lamps and Favrile glass *objets*. The windows in the shop were made by Tiffany to designs by followers of the Nabis, including Pierre Bonnard, Edouard Vuillard and Ker-Xavier Roussel, and set a style that was to take its name from Bing's shop; sadly, these windows are now lost. The Art Nouveau style of stained glass is characterized by its swirling asymmetrical naturalism; clean, sinuous lines often ending in a whiplash; graceful, sensuous female figures, and exaggerated floral and other organic themes. It was considered to have reached its peak at the Exposition Universelle in Paris in 1900, and – although instantly recognizable – Art Nouveau had no strict definition and was more a visual language than a formal statement of design.

In England, Arthur Lasenby Liberty promoted the Art Nouveau style. Associated with Tiffany since the opening of his shop in London's Regent Street in 1875 – and not far from Tiffany & Co's own shop in the same street – Liberty's customers soon included the fashionable decorators of the period, and the style quickly spread. One of Tiffany's most successful but little-known commissions in Great Britain is in the Kirk at Fyvie in Scotland; the window depicts a hauntingly beautiful, young St Michael, and was designed in memory of Percy Forbes-Leith, a young army officer who had died in South Africa in 1900.

Tiffany's work in the United States started to decrease after the early years of this century, and his decline in popularity was accelerated by the First World War. His control of the firm and its high standards began to slip and by 1928, when Tiffany retired from the company, his style was unfashionable, his work regarded as gaudy and dated. This change in taste caused tragic loss of his glass, as it began to be consigned to attics and, worse, rubbish tips. However, the wheel of fashion has again turned full circle, and now Tiffany's work is much admired. Particularly fine examples of his glass are a two-panel window of exotic birds on a balustrade, commissioned by Capt Joseph R Delamar and now in Glen Cove, Long Island; a memorial window in the Christ Episcopal Church, Rye, New York, and the collections in The Metropolitan Museum of Art and the Museum of Modern Art in New York City. There are also extensive collections of Tiffany's work in the Corning Museum of Glass, the Charles Hosmer Morse Foundation in Florida and in the Haworth Art Gallery in Lancashire.

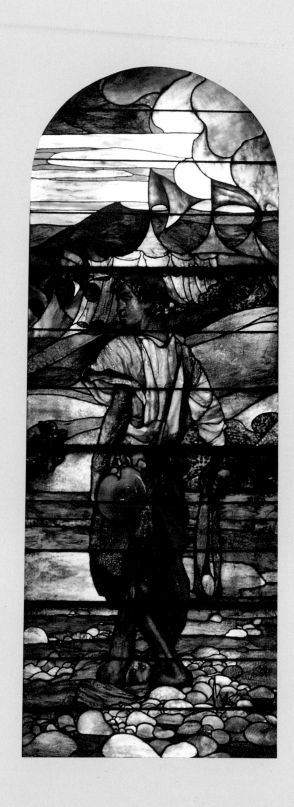

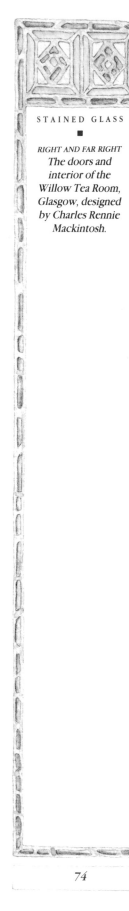

British Glass

AT THE GREAT Exhibition of 1851, Joseph Paxton had astonished everyone with his iron and glass Crystal Palace, which had opened up exciting opportunities as huge metal-ribbed domes and roofs of glass now became structurally possible. New commercial buildings and shops hurried to be fashionable under the influence of the Arts and Crafts Movement and the Art Nouveau style, and stained glass became an essential decorative element in building. Church building too reached a peak, demanding enormous quantities of stained glass to fill its windows, some, regrettably, of inferior quality. At the turn of the century, the vogue for stained glass was at its height; stained-glass door and transom panels became part of every middle-class house in the growing city suburbs, and studios published catalogues of standard designs.

In ecclesiastical windows two themes emerged in stained glass. The first was that produced by followers of the Arts and Crafts Movement, led by Christopher Whall, and later by his pupils, who included Karl Parsons, Henry Payne and Hugh Arnold. These artists, many of them women, developed Whall's tradition of purity of colour and the highest standards of craftsmanship. The second theme was the traditional pictorial one that had been practised by Charles Eamer Kempe and carried on by Ninian Comper and, after him, by such artists as Christopher and Geoffrey Webb and Hugh Easton.

Times, though, were changing. After the turn of the century, new thoughts in architecture – leading to less ornamentation in building – were coming to the fore, while interiors tended towards a less richly coloured and less cluttered look, with larger clear-glazed windows.

At the same time, the decrease in church build-ing reflected changing religious and social habits. Stained glass was no longer in such demand, and this decline led to the demise of the great Victorian studios and closure of many small firms, which was sharply accelerated by the outbreak of war in 1914. In 1915, Alfred Wolmark's window in St Mary's Church, Slough, was one of the first examples of the use of abstract designs in stained glass. This work reflected the begin-nings of Cubist influence in art, but it was to take a long time before any other significant abstract stained-glass work appeared in England.

In Scotland, there was a thriving stained-glass school based in Glasgow, its most notable exponent being the firm of J & W Guthrie. Among those who designed for them were Christopher Whall and the renowned archi-tect Charles Rennie Mackintosh. When the latter in-cluded stained glass as part of his 1896 commission for Miss Cranston's Buchanan Street Tea Rooms, it was Guthries who carried out the work. Mackintosh used the company extensively for his stained glass, which found more recognition in Austria, France and Ger-many than England.

A little-known part of Glasgow's rich stained-glass tradition was the small decorative painted fanlights and door-panel medallions found in the drab tene-ment blocks of that period, of which much, surprisingly, still survives. J Gordon Guthrie Jr, after a family row, left his native city in 1896 for the United States, where he joined the Tiffany Studios. Later he designed for other studios, finally joining fellow Glaswegian Henry Wynd Young in New York, where they gained a considerable reputation for refined new-Gothic-style stained glass. Guthrie's work shows a skilful handling of strong colour, often combined with white, and he became one of the foremost stained glass artists of his day.

The United States

AT THE TURN of the century in the United States, opalescent glass was paramount. An architectural renaissance was under way, with an emphasis towards elegant classicism using strong, clear lines.

Architects were building with marble and limestone in a grand manner for rich clients, such as the Vanderbilts, and the gentle tones of opalescent glass – its surfaces reflecting and refracting light – blended well with the new materials. The figures depicted in the windows became very grand and heroic, angels developed huge eagle-like wings, and the rich colours and swirling figural and plant forms naturally led into the restless curviform line of the Art Nouveau period. Ecclesiastical stained glass generally remained true to the Gothic tradition, although Louis Comfort Tiffany

designed many of his distinctive windows for churches.

In the very early years of the 20th century, there appeared a more functional style of architecture that was concerned with space and form. The style was pioneered by Frank Lloyd Wright, who used stained glass as a screen between the inside and the outside, allowing the light and view to reach the interior of his houses. His windows have fine dominant lead lines of abstract and geometric shapes in harmony with the building, and they use colour sparingly. Much of his stained glass was made by the Linden Glass Company of Chicago, including that for perhaps his most successful architectural stained glass, in the Dana-Thomas house, built in 1904 in Springfield, Illinois. Wright's concepts were taken up

in Europe, particularly in Germany, where his influence inspired a later generation of stained-glass artists, including Josef Albers. It is interesting that one of the greatest American architects instigated a radical and exciting new concept in the architectural use of glass.

By the entry of the United States into the Great War in Europe, the vogue for opalescent glass was on the wane. The enthusiasm for building huge houses for the rich, decorated by stained glass, flagged as the price of land rose and apartments and small houses in the cheaper suburbs became the new wave of building. Stained glass in this context gave way to natural light and views, and, coupled with a reaction against the use of so much stained glass, it became unfashionable and unwanted.

European Art Nouveau

MANY EUROPEAN stained-glass artists disparagingly referred to opalescent glass as 'American glass', and continued to use their pot-metal colours and antique glass. In France, the artists of the Ecole de Nancy gave Art Nouveau a new meaning when their master glazier, Jacques Gruber, adapted a new method of superimposing layers of colour onto white glass, thus producing a whole new palette of colours. The process was much used by Emile Gallé, especially for his vases.

Many countries were influenced by or developed their own distinctive styles of Art Nouveau. In Spain, Antonio Gaudí was admired for his highly individual work for the rich Spanish industrialist Count Don Eusebio Güell at his Barcelona palace, where flower-shaped rose windows adorned the family chapel. In Belgium, Victor Horta carried the concept into his architecture and stained glass, while another Belgian, Henry van de Velde, sold stained glass in direct rivalry to Bing. In Europe, however, as in the United States, the wheel of fashion and a surfeit of stained glass led to an increasing decline in work; the outbreak of the Great War nearly ended it completely.

■

FAR LEFT (*DETAIL*) *AND LEFT* **This Annunciation window, designed by Arild Rosenkranz and John La Farge and made of opalescent glass, was the first to be produced in the United States for the European market. Wickhambreaux Church, Kent.**

BELOW **Three-light window designed by Edward Burne-Jones for Morris & Co, 1869. Cheddleton, Staffordshire.**

THE BREAK IN ECCLESIASTICAL TRADITION

Design for a window in Robinson College, Cambridge, by John Piper.

RIGHT *Window by Jan Thorn Prikker, in the Church of the Three Kings in Neuss, W Germany, 1920s.*

 ON THE HEELS of the end of the First World War in 1918 came social upheaval and economic depression. It was neither a time for encouraging artistic talent nor for funding major new commissions. Viewed as a whole, the years between the wars were unremarkable for stained glass, yet it was at this time that the seeds of revolutionary ideas were sown by, among others, Georges Rouault in France and Jan Thorn Prikker in Germany. Suppressed by World War II, these seeds sprang into life in the postwar years, blossoming into a dynamic talent in the rebuilt churches and cathedrals of Europe.

In the United States, enthusiasm for opalescent glass had already died, and a neo-Gothic style was re-established. There, as in Europe, an intellectual and aesthetic struggle developed to find a way out of the apparent confinement of the stereotyped tradition of pictorial ecclesiastical windows. The release found in abstraction and symbolism was in many cases expressed by artists who were not practising Christians, and whose glass found other ways to express new purpose in the Church, such as by representing peace or calm and order in a rapidly changing world. Christian artists too began to express spirituality in this new art form, and a whole new concept in stained glass spread through European and American churches.

However, the traditional pictorial style incorporating beautiful translucent pot-metal glass and painting has continued, in Germany only barely surviving, but in England and the United States still widely popular. In the first part of the century, though, it was in the Republic of Ireland that some of the richest of this traditional talent emerged, centred mainly in the south.

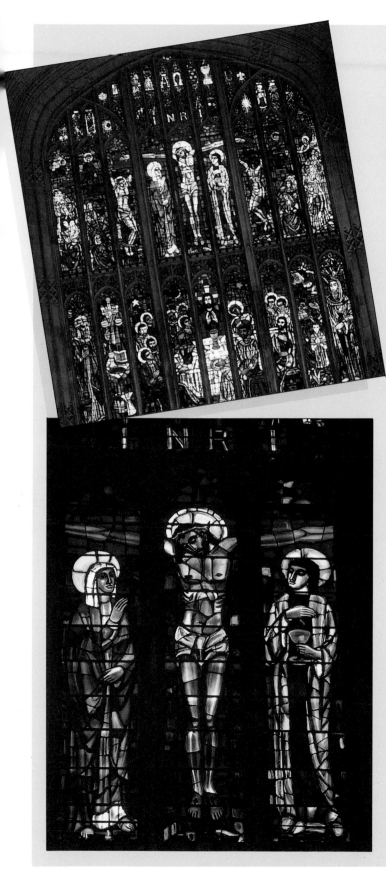

IN DUBLIN in 1903, An Túr Gloine (the Tower of Glass), a cooperative-style studio similar to the Glass House in London, was founded by Edward Martyn and Sarah Purser. Martyn was a patron of the Abbey Theatre, Purser a successful portrait painter who, at 50, was to continue her involvement with stained glass until the grand age of 93. They chose as their manager Alfred Child, an ex-pupil of Christopher Whall, and encouraged a medieval approach, with bold use of colour and strong careful painting. At the studios they gathered together a number of gifted artists, including Wilhelmina Geddes, Harry Clarke, Michael Healy and Evie Hone.

Wilhelmina Geddes joined An Túr Gloine in 1912, working under the tuition of Alfred Child. Among her many successful early windows was one made in 1919 for Ottawa in memory of the Duke of Connaught. In 1925, she set up her own studio in London, where, in spite of recurring poor health, she carried out some of her finest work – notably the great *Te Deum* War Memorial window of 1938, which Great Britain presented to the Belgian Government for St Martin's Cathedral, Ypres.

Harry Clarke was an outstanding illustrator of books as well as a successful stained-glass artist. He came from a family of church decorators and received his early training from Alfred Child at Dublin's Metropolitan School of Art. His use of rich colours in his windows is distinctive, often mixing pinks, bright greens, purples and blues. There is a certain lyrical quality about his work, such as in his window of *The Nativity* for the Church of Ireland at Castlelaugh, County Cork. He took immense care in his work, sometimes firing a single piece of glass several times over until he was satisfied, and never once relaxing his high standards. Probably his greatest work was the Last Judgement with the Blessed Virgin Mary and St Patrick, for the Catholic Church of Newport, County Mayo, completed shortly before his death in 1931 aged 42.

Evie Hone was an abstract painter who became interested in stained glass on her frequent visits to France; her first windows, made in 1934, indicate a remarkable skill. The influence of the French artist Georges Rouault and her enthusiasm for Irish medieval carvings and sculpture are apparent in many of her windows. Her most famous international commission was the large *Crucifixion and Last Supper* in the east window of Eton College Chapel, which took three years to complete. She died in 1955, 11 years after An Túr Gloine had been dissolved.

ABOVE AND LEFT **The east window of Eton College Chapel was executed by Evie Hone at her studio in Rathfarnham, County Dublin, 1949–52.**

American Gothic

IN THE FIRST part of the 20th century, ecclesiastical stained glass in the United States was largely and closely modelled on medieval glass in Europe. Outstanding examples are the many windows in the enormous neo-Gothic cathedrals of St John the Divine in New York City, and St Peter and St Paul in Washington.

By the beginning of the century, the richly coloured opalescent glass landscapes in ecclesiastical architecture were anathema to a new generation of architects who rejected the mixing and abasement of different styles in Victorian building, and sought a purity based on true Gothic principles. This purity extended to the stained glass that they planned for their churches. Foremost among these architects was Ralph Adams Cram, whose writings and lectures were summarized in his book published in 1936, *My Life in Architecture*. Cram was appointed architect of St John the Divine, begun in 1892, which was the largest Gothic cathedral in the world, and filled with English glass.

There was a long precedent for using English stained-glass studios to make ecclesiastical windows, and this custom continued while the vogue for opalescent glass waxed and then waned. When the choir and two chapels of St John the Divine were consecrated in 1911,

CHAPTER SIX

■

LEFT AND BELOW LEFT
**Dalle de verre (or
slab glass) stained-
glass windows by
Fernand Léger
showing large
organic forms
interwined with
Christian symbols,
1950–52. Church
of the Sacred
Heart, Audincourt,
France.**

the windows were from England, by Hardmans, Powell and Clayton & Bell. They were fine examples, particularly the upper window behind the high altar of Christ in Glory by James Powell, and Clayton & Bell's St Columba Chapel window, based on the grisaille work in York Minster; but they were Victorian in style and execution. This was perhaps the high point of Victorian ecclesiastical glass in the United States, for in that same year Cram set about creating a pure French Gothic style in St John the Divine. He required of his stained glass that same unbroken symmetry in style and use of translucent pot-metal colour that made Chartres so much admired. His search for a suitable stained-glass studio began in England, but there were already American stained-glass artists who were advocating the same principles as Cram.

William Willet was a New York-born stained-glass artist who had worked under John La Farge, and studied medieval glass in Europe. When he met Charles J Connick, a newspaper cartoonist who embraced stained glass as matching his ideals and his talents, they became propagandists for a new generation of neo-Gothic stained-glass artists. Others included Gordon Guthrie, originally from Glasgow, and another Scotsman, Henry Wynd Young. Willet opened his own studio in Philadelphia, and was followed by his son, Henry Lee Willet;

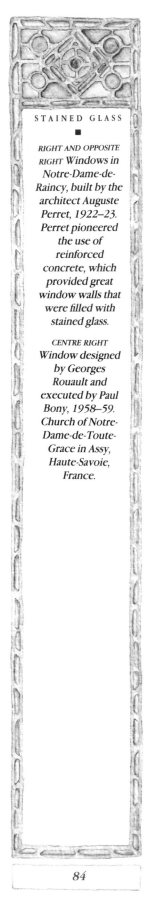

RIGHT AND OPPOSITE RIGHT Windows in Notre-Dame-de-Raincy, built by the architect Auguste Perret, 1922–23. Perret pioneered the use of reinforced concrete, which provided great window walls that were filled with stained glass.

CENTRE RIGHT Window designed by Georges Rouault and executed by Paul Bony, 1958–59. Church of Notre-Dame-de-Toute-Grace in Assy, Haute-Savoie, France.

their studio grew into one of the largest and most respected in the United States. Connick's windows often contain a predominance of blue, regarded by him and other neo-medievalists as almost mystical, and his superb rose window for St John the Divine and his colossal window in St Vincent Ferrer in New York both testify to his belief.

Another talented artist at this time was the son of Cram's partner, Wright Goodhue, who was sadly to commit suicide at the age of 26. Among his many fine windows are those in the baptistry of the Riverside Church in Manhattan. The beautiful blue background enriches the ruby glass, and strong lead lines emphasize the design. It was this church that perhaps witnessed the apogee of neo-Gothic stained glass in 1929, when a copy of the St James's window from the clerestory at Chartres was supplied by a French studio. It was in France, though, that a new interpretation of ecclesiastical stained glass was emerging.

CHAPTER SIX

■

BELOW LEFT
*Window by
Georges Braque in
the Maeght
Museum, St Paul de
Vance, France.*

RIGHT AND OPPOSITE BELOW **Windows by Fernand Léger in Biot, France.**

The Beginnings of Modern Stained Glass in France

ECCLESIASTICAL STAINED glass in France suffered considerably in both world wars. Medieval windows were removed to safety or covered up for protection, leaving the less esteemed 19th-century glass to take its chance. Inevitably, many churches and cathedrals were totally destroyed and many of those left standing lost much of their glass. Between the wars, stained-glass artists banded together in craft workshops to concentrate on the restoration of the damaged glass and to exchange ideas on new glass, of which perhaps the best known was the Atelier d'Art Sacré, founded in 1919.

One of the most respected studios was that of Jean Hébert-Stevens, who advocated a break with the old style, still regarded by many of the clergy as a vehicle for teaching (as it had been in medieval times). When asked to carry out a commission for the church at the Ossuaire de Douaumont near Verdun in 1927, he employed Georges Desvallières as the designer. He had been encouraged in this by the influential Dominican Father Marie-Alain Couturier, who was co-author of the Journal *Art Sacré*. In 1937, Father Couturier invited a number of well-known modern artists, including Georges Rouault, to make designs for the chapel of Notre-Dame-de-Toute-Grace at Assy in Haute-Savoie. The result was a startling, if controversial, new interpretation of religious stained glass, though not entirely

LEFT Braques' window shows a use of bold, vivid colours and flat shapes. Church of St Dominique, Varangeville, France.

successful because of the differing styles. Father Couturier was heavily criticized for turning the church into an exhibition of modern profane art, but after he died in 1954, Marc Chagall was commissioned to make further designs for the baptistry windows.

The experiment at Assy was the beginning of abstract art in religious stained glass. It is interesting that the International Exhibition of that same year was dominated by the work of the traditional studios, whose detailed figures of saints in the new windows for the cathedral of Notre Dame were already being regarded as dated and dull. However, at the 1939 Exposition des Arts Décoratifs at the Petit Palais, work by such new modern artists as Jean Bazaine, Roger Bissiers and Francis Gruber was widely acclaimed.

RIGHT **Three windows by Jean Cocteau in St Maximin, Metz, France.**

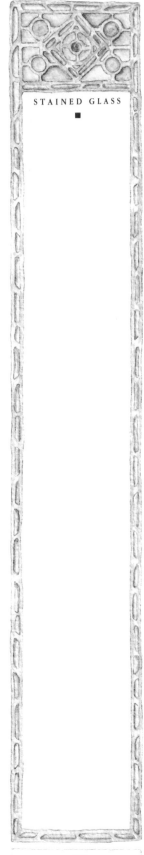
MARC CHAGALL

MARC CHAGALL was 70 years old when his first stained-glass windows were installed at Assy in 1957. This remarkable man stands independently of other stained-glass artists working after the war, and his unique contributions to the art made a dramatic and lasting impact.

Born Moyshe Shagall in 1877 in Russia, he left his hometown and set off for Paris in 1911, carrying with him all the mysticism and influence of the icons that he must have seen in his Russian upbringing. In Paris, he was influenced by Cubism and the Impressionist painters, particularly Gauguin and Van Gogh. He returned to Russia in 1914 to marry his childhood sweetheart, Bella, and did not return to Paris until 1923, where his painting, ceramic decoration and lithographs found wide acclaim. His swirling dream-like imagery resulted from his view of life – 'I am a mystic. I don't go to church or to the synagogue. For me working is praying'.

ABOVE LEFT A memorial window to Sarah D'Avigdor-Goldsmid — one of 12 windows designed by Marc Chagall and executed by Charles and Brigitte Marcq of the Atelier Jacques Simon in Reims for All Saints Church, Tudeley, Kent.

ABOVE A memorial window to Dag Hammarskjöld, former Secretary-General of the United Nations, designed by Marc Chagall for the United Nations building in New York. It is predominantly blue and strewn with coloured images representing peace.

Following Assy, his next important commission was for the cathedral at Metz between 1960 and 1965. Here, as in all his windows, the problem of translating his work into glass was entrusted to Charles and Brigitte Marcq in Reims. The Marcqs carefully and laboriously met his colour requirements and by painting, aciding and etching, they faithfully created his floating forms and bold lines in glass, paint and lead. In 1962, he produced 12 windows for the Hadassah Medical Centre in Jerusalem, where, to avoid portraying the human figure (forbidden in Judaic art), he used symbols and animals with human characteristics. His window for the United Nations in memory of Dag Hammarskjöld is an essay in blue, a favourite colour of his, which he used again in his beautiful memorial window in All Saints Church, Tudeley, Kent, to Sarah d'Avigdor-Goldsmid, who was drowned in a sailing accident.

The Influence of Jan Thorn Prikker

THORN PRIKKER was Dutch by birth, but worked and taught in Germany and was, like his counterparts in France, principally an abstract painter. His work in stained glass uses dynamic elements in simplified pictorial form, sometimes, as in his panel *Orange* of 1931, limited to one plane. Similar experiments in glass grew from the influential Bauhaus school, where Theo Van Doesburg, Paul Klee and Josef Albers were involved with its stained-glass department (unfortunately, little of their work survived the war). Thorn Prikker's work created enormous interest in a new generation of German stained-glass artists who carried their work into the 1950s, principally Anton Wendling, Heinrich Camperdonk and Georg Meistermann. Like the French craftsmen, Meistermann was veering away from figurative glass. His work was to reach its peak with his windows in the Church of St Maria-im-Kapital, where his use of paint was minimal and the composition of the windows displayed a great freedom of style. His then-revolutionary windows in 1938 for the Church of St Engelbert at Solingen in the Ruhr were sadly destroyed in the war.

Anton Wendling made his home before the war in Aachen, where in 1949 he designed huge abstract windows in geometric patterns for the choir in Aachen Cathedral. His windows tend to comprise a repeating geometric pattern, often referred to as tiered coloured masonry. In 1947, when teaching at the Technical University, he engaged as his assistant a young artist called Ludwig Schaffrath, who was to be one of the greatest postwar stained-glass artists in Europe.

Postwar German Ecclesiastical Glass

AFTER THE terrible destruction of World War II, church building in Germany presented a unique opportunity for the new stained-glass artists, many influenced by Jan Thorn Prikker's abstract style and believing that ecclesiastical glass need not necessarily depict biblical stories. Glass became monochromatic in colour and graphic in composition, completely filling large openings and creating a comprehensive unity between windows and wall.

Another outstanding artist of the postwar years who, like Schaffrath, has dispensed almost completely with painted work – except occasional subtle shading, using the leads to delineate line – is Johannes Schreiter. His blue opalescent glass at the Johannesbund Chapel at Leutesdorf is an essay in windows which are a part of, rather than in, the architecture. In 1969, he designed 33 windows for St Marien in Dortmund, where all the original glass had been destroyed in the war. Fortunately, the beautiful altar painting of 1420 by Konrad von Soest survived and forms the focal point in the apse, with the new windows uniting the different architectural styles of the building, i.e., Romanesque, High Gothic and Modern.

A contemporary of Schaffrath and Schreiter is Jochem Poensgen, whose development of simplified form and line to integrate with the architecture of the church can be seen at Christ Kerk Dinslaken and St Jacob in Reuthe/Vorarlberg. The work of these, and other German postwar ecclesiastical artists, has proved prolific and international.

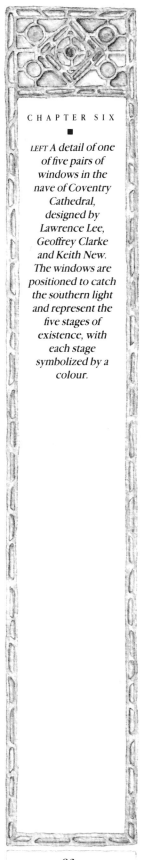

LEFT A detail of one of five pairs of windows in the nave of Coventry Cathedral, designed by Lawrence Lee, Geoffrey Clarke and Keith New. The windows are positioned to catch the southern light and represent the five stages of existence, with each stage symbolized by a colour.

APART FROM Alfred Wolmark's early experiment in abstract composition in 1915 at St Mary's, Slough, commissioned by Mr Ellerman of Ellerman's Embrocation fame, England between the wars kept safely to its pictorial painterly tradition in stained glass. The work of A K Nicholson, Martin Travers and Hugh Easton was in this tradition, though individual in style, as was that of Christopher Webb, whose postwar Shakespeare window in Southwark Cathedral is much admired. At the end of the war, although many churches in southern England had been damaged by bombing, there was nothing like the opportunity for new commissions that existed in Germany. Much of the new glass looked backwards, and although generally of high quality, owed nothing to the contemporary work then being carried out on the Continent. It was the rebuilding of Coventry Cathedral and the new Roman Catholic Cathedral in Liverpool that revolutionized stained glass in England.

Destroyed by bombing during the war, Coventry Cathedral was rebuilt by the architect Sir Basil Spence, using concrete and glass with the new building linked to the remains of the old. The nave windows – 70 in all – were angled to catch the southern light and visible in their entirety only from the altar end. Designed by Lawrence Lee, Geoffrey Clarke and Keith New, they represent, through symbolic use of colour, the relationship between God and Man at different stages in Man's life. They were a radical break with tradition, but it was the huge curved window in the baptistry by John Piper that created the greatest controversy when the cathedral was consecrated in 1962, and is now accepted as a landmark in British stained-glass design. A great sunburst of colour reaching from floor to ceiling, the window symbolizes the light of the Holy Spirit breaking through into the world. Surrounding the central blaze of yellow and white rectangles are abstract patterns in purples, blues, reds, greens, browns, ochres and greys. More in the French than the English tradition, John Piper the artist made the design and the cartoon, but left the interpretation into glass to Patrick Reyntiens.

Their earliest windows, installed in Oundle School Chapel in 1956, of nine symbolic knights in vivid colour and with strong curvilinear painting and leading, are still considered by many to be among their best work, as well as a watershed in English stained glass. Following Coventry, Piper and Reyntiens were given the commission for the great lantern tower in Liverpool Cathedral (1965–67): the abstract design in *dalle de*

OPPOSITE Window in the Basilika of St Gereon, Cologne, by Georg Meistermann.

FAR LEFT One of three Gothic-style windows in Oundle Chapel, Northamptonshire. They were John Piper's first stained-glass commission and represent the nine aspects of Christ. They were executed by Patrick Reyntiens in 1955.

LEFT The domed lantern in the Metropolitan Cathedral of Christ the King, Liverpool, by John Piper and Patrick Reyntiens, symbolizing the Trinity in three bursts of colour.

verre crowns the inside of the cathedral by day, and, when lit at night, it is like a spectacular lighthouse of colour from the outside. Among their many successful later works are the chancel windows for the chapel of Robinson College, Cambridge. Other English artists working at this time included Brian Thomas, Margaret Traherne, Francis Skeat, Keith New and Arthur Buss, who designed the enormous heraldic rose window at Lancing College in Sussex, the largest built in Europe since the Reformation.

American Slab Glass

POSTWAR ECCLESIASTICAL glass in the United States suffered initially from honest but weak and sometimes insipid variations of the neo-Gothic style. In fairness to the studios and artists working during these years, it was the Church that demanded windows depicting traditional imagery, but also insisting that the brightness of daylight be allowed to pour through. It was a situation that fed on itself: disappointing stained glass led to fewer commissions, a reluctance to experiment, and

more disappointing windows. An escape from this impasse came with the use of *dalle de verre*, literally, slab of glass. Developed and much used in France, it first appeared in North America in 1939 at the New York World's Fair, although the popularity of this slab glass did not catch the public imagination until much later. Its rich colour and angular shape lent it to abstract design, and because it was comparatively cheap and structural in form, it became economic to use in large spectacular walls of glass.

One of the earliest examples of slab glass on a large scale was at the First Presbyterian Church in Stamford, Connecticut, in 1958: designed by the French stained-glass artist Gabriel Loire, the inclined walls became the windows, stretching from floor to roof. In this case, the slabs of glass were set into concrete; recently, epoxy resin has been much used, giving equivalent strength but lighter weight to the structure. Later examples include St Mary Mother of Jesus Church in Brooklyn and the huge windows by Judson Studios in the Air Force Academy Chapel, New Colorado Springs, where the glass is set into metal.

■

RIGHT Window in Robinson College, Cambridge, by John Piper and Patrick Reyntiens.

OPPOSITE ABOVE This Romanesque-style composition by John Piper and Patrick Reyntiens portrays the Adoration of the Magi, flanked by trumpeting angels with two pagan monsters beneath their feet. Below are Adam and Eve, and on the right The Last Supper. Robinson College. Cambridge, 1982.

■

BELOW LEFT *The First Presbyterian Church, Stamford, Connecticut, built in 1958. The walls are composed of pre-cast concrete panels. The nave walls are of glass, stretching from the floor to the roof and made up of multifaceted triangular panels; designed by Gabriel Loire.*

BELOW *The largest rose window in Britain was designed by Arthur Buss and fabricated by Goddard & Gibbs. Lancing College, Sussex.*

Chapter Seven

PUBS TO PALACES

A huge multi-coloured dome in the Royal Pavilion
of the Malaz Stadium, Riyadh, Saudi Arabia,
designed by Alan Younger and executed by
Goddard & Gibbs Studios.

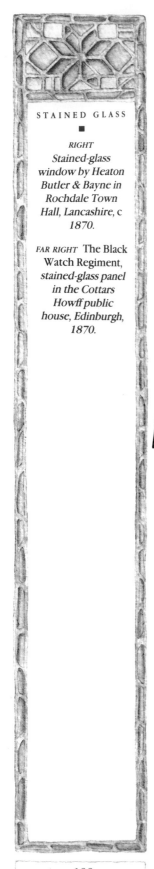

 STAINED GLASS HAS traditionally been a Christian art rooted in the great medieval ecclesiastical buildings of Europe, with the Church its principal patron and religion its inspiration. When domestic and public buildings first had glazed windows, these were normally in the form of leaded lights – the term for small rectangles or diamonds of glass set in a grid of lead cames. This pattern work resulted from the small panes of flat glass it was then possible to cut, and the fragility of the material itself, with some glass perhaps only .08 in/2 mm thick. By the 16th century, quite elaborate lead light patterns were appearing, sometimes also incorporating stained glass, most commonly as a heraldic device. This use of stained glass, however, was seldom found outside great houses or important public buildings, and it was not until the 19th century that its use became widespread.

The rapid growth of a neo-Gothic style of architecture, together with aspirations to public grandeur and private status, created a demand for secular stained glass. As the century progressed, lavish embellishments and decoration were employed in building: elaborate

RIGHT West
German Radio
Station in Cologne
by George
Meistermann. This
huge window,
called Colour
Tones of Music,
caused a great stir
when installed in
1952.

wood, stone and brick-work windows incorporated equally elaborate stained glass. Its early use was purely decorative, with little deference to a building's style or function, and the control and influence of light in an interior were often subordinated to a virtuoso, occasionally overwhelming, display of coloured glass. Examples of this can still be found in many of the remaining large buildings of the Victorian age. In the United States, the work of the celebrated architect Louis Sullivan in Chicago after the 1871 fire has all the confidence associated with the richly ornamented architecture of this period. He extensively used decorative glass, notably in his 1893–4 Stock Exchange building and in his last great work, the Carson, Pine & Scott department store. Undoubtedly, Sullivan and his more famous former employee, Frank Lloyd Wright, understood the sympathetic and functional use of stained glass in their buildings.

In England the great town hall in the city of Rochdale, built by W H Crosland in 1871 in the fashionable Gothic style, is a fine example of the compelling richness of massed decorative stained glass. Similar examples abounded in both North America and Europe, although much has now disappeared with the destruction of war and the rebuilding of the cities.

In the suburban house-building boom at the turn of the century, it was the front door and the front parlour windows that contained stained glass, both as a form of window dressing and, sometimes together with the drawn net curtains, as a form of privacy. Art Nouveau and its successor Art Deco influenced the simple designs of such windows, and it is interesting how the fashion for decorative glazing that started in the major towns gradually spread over a number of years to other parts of the country. As communications improved, so changes in fashion and style that affected decorative glass became more universal: what had previously evolved over many years now became widely written about and photographed.

Art Deco

IN THE YEARS between the start of this century and the First World War, stained glass was beginning to lose its appeal. Frank Lloyd Wright's Prairie-style houses were in some respects an end and not a beginning, and younger architects and fashionable designers turned away from the earlier excessive use of coloured glass. In 1904, President Theodore Roosevelt ordered the breaking up of Tiffany's opalescent screen in the White House, and everywhere secular stained-glass commissions were increasingly harder to find.

Art Nouveau decoration was similarly losing its

appeal, and being replaced by a new style called Art Deco, which was the antithesis of free-flowing naturalistic line. Its new strong geometry and angular patterns particularly suited the move toward a less ostentatious and more functional architectural style, which was appearing.

The popularity of Art Deco stained glass was much more evident in the United States than in Europe, where it spanned the move away from opalescent glass and the decline of the Tiffany Studios, to the use of translucent glass and a new generation of artists and studios. Perhaps the most notable Art Deco windows – principally ecclesiastical – were produced by the new Rambusch Studios in New York.

Building in Glass

IN EUROPE, as in the United States, stained glass was seldom used in commercial buildings after the First World War, and in the new vogue for plainness in domestic interiors, it was regarded as old-fashioned and an obstruction to light and view. Glass, though, while no longer used as a decorative element in building, began to play an increasingly important role in architecture.

As early as 1829, glass had been used as architecture in Fontaine's Galerie d'Orléans, while later Joseph Paxton's 1851 Crystal Palace in London had paved the way for Taut's Glass Pavilion for the 1914 Cologne Werkbund Exhibition, which came close to realizing the German Expressionists' dream of a 'Crystal City'. In the same year, Paul Scheerbart's book *Glasarchitektur* heightened interest in the use of glass as a building material.

This had been made possible by the development of steel framing as the load-bearing element of a building, which allowed the outer walls to be infilled with glass. American skyscrapers epitomized this revolution in building technique. At the same time, developments in the production of flat glass – particularly the ability to produce very large sheets of plate glass – and of glass-related products such as Vitrolite allowed the cladding of steel frame-construction buildings with glass. In 1930s London, the Peter Jones department store and *Daily Express* newspaper offices were the forerunners of Foster Associates' Sainsbury Arts Centre in Norwich (1975–78), while Richard Rogers' use of 'sparkle' glass in the new Lloyds Insurance building in the City of London was inspired by Pierre Chareau's too-little-known 1928 Maison de Verre in Paris. It is, however, Mies Van Der Rohe's Lever House in New York, built in 1952, which has a good claim to be the first truly glass building.

CHAPTER SEVEN

■

BELOW LEFT Jan Thorn Prikker's first commission, Hagen Railway Station, W Germany, 1911.

RIGHT Art Nouveau
window in the
Queen's Head
public house,
Crouch End,
London.

STAINED GLASS

■

RIGHT Lever House, New York City, by the architect Miles Van Der Rohe, 1952, is acknowledged as the first truly glass building.

Decorative Glass

WHILE GLASS was being developed as a building material, it continued to play a part in architectural and interior decoration, but not necessarily as stained glass. Glass used decoratively without colour was nothing new. The process of engraving and embossing glass had been known before the 19th century, but as taxes were removed and flat glass became cheaper, so new trades appeared concerned with its decoration. Engraving glass involves cutting into the surface with a sharp instrument, often a diamond point, or cutting a pattern with a revolving stone wheel, a process known as brilliant cutting. Embossing involves the use of dilute hydrofluoric acid to burn into the surface of the glass: by adding chemically to the acid, degrees of obscuration can be achieved, a process known as 'French embossing', after its discovery in France in the second half of the 19th century. By building up layers of acid-etching, it is possible to achieve complex tonal and surface effects, thus allowing pictures and scenes to be created, as well as lettering and linear decoration.

The art of interior glass work is probably seen at its best in the English pub. The pub, or 'public house', is an institution: its origins lie in medieval monastic refreshment, which, following the dissolution of the monasteries in the 16th century, progressed from houses selling homemade beer and identified by a sign outside, to major breweries setting up chains of 'public houses' in the growing cities. To meet the approval of the licensing magistrates and the moral indignation of the growing middle classes, the brewers' architects vied with each other for respectability through their designs. Ambitious glass decoration, also often involving gilding and painting, filled the new pubs, with stained glass and mirrors adding to the richness of the effect. At much the same time, this form of glass decoration began to appear in hotels and some shops, but its legacy remains in the surviving pubs of the big cities. In London, the Balmoral Castle in Pimlico and the Lord Nelson in the Old Kent Road are fine surviving early examples.

Toward the end of the century, a method of silvering over painting on the glass made possible back-painted glass mirrors; those in the Tottenham in London's Oxford Street remain in place today. One of the largest and most successful London companies producing decorative glass work was that of Walter Gibbs and Sons, which started in 1861 in Southwark, and some of whose signed mirrors installed in 1896 can still be seen in the Half Moon at Herne Hill. Their descendant, Goddard and Gibbs Studios, still carries out elaborate decorative glass work. Another famous London company involved in this work went under the intriguing

name of Cakebread, Robey & Co; their best surviving work is in the Salisbury in Harringay, where they originally also supplied the stained glass, now sadly lost.

Sandblasting is a different decorating technique, where the surface of the glass is abraded by bombardment with air-driven particles of silica. The size of the silica grit determines the coarseness of the effect, which can vary from a fine shading on the glass surface to deep moulding producing a three-dimensional appearance. A much easier and safer medium to work with than acids, it is becoming an increasingly popular form of glass decoration. While England and France may be the traditional homes of decorative flat glass, it is in the United States that the most exciting and imaginative work is now to be found, with studios such as Bolae in Florida creating the most beautiful work, on screens and tables as well as windows.

The bevelling of glass, wherein the perimeter is ground to produce a sloping edge, remains popular as a decorative feature in windows and internal screens. Almost any shape of glass can be bevelled, giving an attractive sparkle as the light is reflected and refracted

in many directions. Bevels are often combined with mirror backing or stained glass to increase the effect. Aciding, brilliant cutting, back painting, sandblasting and bevelling have all become highly skilled individual trades, involving long apprenticeships. When labour was cheap and a craftsman's commitment was for life, they were relatively inexpensive processes, but in today's changed circumstances they have become a rare skill.

The Beginnings of a New Approach

IN THE INTERWAR years, as secular commissions reduced to a trickle, all the leading stained-glass artists had become heavily dependent on the patronage of the Church. Many of the old studios disappeared in bankruptcy and closure. The story on the two continents was the same, as most countries suffered postwar economic depression, as well as political and social unrest: it was a barren climate for new stained glass. Little innovative modern design was attempted as churches demanded variations on the theme of traditional ecclesiastical windows. Nevertheless, in Germany there appeared the stirrings of a fresh and vital new approach to stained glass.

Theo Van Doesburg and Josef Albers, who were both involved with the Bauhaus School, were two important figures in stained glass between the wars. The latter's screen windows, made for Walter Gropius's Sommerfeld House in Berlin in the early 1920s, typified the Bauhaus philosophy of the integration of architecture, materials and social needs. More lasting and influential was the work of Jan Thorn Prikker, the abstract painter who later turned to stained glass and developed a pure style of simplified colour and form. After his death in 1932, Anton Wendling, who worked both figuratively and non-figuratively, and Heinrich Camperdonk continued the influence of German abstract stained glass, taking it into its dominant position in the postwar years.

CHAPTER SEVEN

■

LEFT AND BELOW LEFT
Exterior and interior view of Georg Meistermann's 'Bottrop Spiral' – a milestone in the history of stained glass, 1958.

STAINED GLASS

■

RIGHT Two of a series of six windows designed for St Antonius Hospital Chapel in Eschweiler, W Germany, by Ludwig Schaffrath in 1976. They are in sharp contrast to his more formal geometric-style windows.

BELOW RIGHT Exterior view of a window designed by Schaffrath for the entrance hall of a swimming pool in Ubach-Palenberg, W Germany, 1973.

CHAPTER SEVEN

■

LEFT This window in St Mary's Church, Köln Kalk, W Germany, is an unusual blend of abstraction and realism. Designed by Georg Meistermann.

Postwar German Glass

THE ENORMOUS destruction wrought in Germany by the war meant a massive rebuilding programme, whose scale and speed encouraged experiments in architecture and decoration. Coupled with this was a taxation system sympathetic to donors of public art, and legislation requiring such work in new buildings. The opportunity for mediocrity – if only through repetitiveness because of the sheer volume of work required – was obvious, but on the whole this was triumphantly overcome. Surprisingly, it was the Church that led the way: keen to replace an image of an imperial and Nazi past with that of a social democratic future, it welcomed the abstract stained glass pioneered before the war.

The early leader was Georg Meistermann, who formed the link between the prewar and postwar German stained-glass artists. His huge window for the West German radio station at Cologne in 1952 caused a sensation. His window at the church in Bottrop –

CHAPTER SEVEN
■

LEFT **Window by
Wilhelm Buschulte
in St Peter's
Church, Aachen,
W Germany.**

known as the 'spiral' – is considered a landmark in postwar stained-glass design. Other talented German stained-glass artists include Wilhelm Buschulte, whose work emphasizes delicate overall pattern, and Joachim Klos and Jochem Poensgen, who each executed one of the entry wall windows for the Police Academy at Munster-Hilltrup in 1983, with large monochromatic areas of glass and a graphic use of lead lines, typical of postwar German stained glass.

Arguably the two greatest artists of this period are Ludwig Schaffrath and Johannes Schreiter. Much of the work they have produced is ecclesiastical, and has been executed by a commercial studio providing an exact interpretation of the artist's wishes, the best known being Derix Glass Studio in Taunusstein. This relationship is rare outside Germany, where the artist/craftsman or studio designer is almost invariably found, or the even rarer partnership of artist and craftsman. Ludwig Schaffrath was born in Alsdorf in 1924 and his childhood among the pits possibly influenced him in his use

of black lead lines against pale windows. His glass contributes to the architecture of a building, using quiet tones and ordered line, and, by emphasizing linear form, it links the stained glass to the building. His use of colour is sparing, but when he does use it, it becomes a balance to other action in the window. The rippling effect of water in his swimming-pool entrance hall window at Ubach-Palenberg of 1973 – with its small 'jewels' of colours – is typical of the effectiveness of his compositions from both inside and outside.

Johannes Schreiter, like Schaffrath, rarely uses paint and employs lead lines and glass in a free abstract form to give a feeling of floating movement and spontaneity. However, his windows are still part of the building, never trying to make a statement except in harmony with the architecture. His early windows in the choir of Exerzitienhaus Chapel, Johannesbund, are a superb symphony in glass: among his best known international work are the windows he executed for Notre Dame in Douai, France (1975–77).

WHILE IN Germany stained glass was developing into a truly postwar movement, in France, and to a lesser extent in England, a group of distinguished artists was 'painting in glass'. They were a prewar generation who were first and foremost artists and who approached their subject with the painter's eye, rather than as designer/craftsmen. Their work was interpreted by craftsmen who, working very closely with them, translated their designs into glass, paint and lead, thereby producing some of the most beautiful stained glass of the postwar years. They used the brightness of the light coming through the glass instead of being reflected from their canvas, and turned the disciplines of painting and leading to their advantage by refusing to be imprisoned by tradition. Their reference was painting and they always turned back to it for refreshment and inspiration. Craft was important to them, but when it became overworked in pursuit of excellence, they saw it as leading to conformity and mediocrity.

This relationship of artist and craftsman was strongest in France with Georges Braque and Paul Bony, Chagall and the Marcqs, Henri Matisse and again Bony, and Fernand Léger and Barillet. In England, it flourished with the work of John Piper and Patrick Reyntiens. In France, there was a history of liberalism, both in the Church's spiritual and intellectual approach to art and in the commissioning of private work. This allowed a church to have a window expressing humanity without being strictly Christian in design or execution, and thus a non-believer could express peace without the necessity of an angel or a saint.

In England, the attitude was different, with the Church looking back to the comfortable status quo of calmer, earlier years and an ordered society. Their stained-glass commissions were, with few exceptions, for safe traditional windows, resulting in excellent craftsmanship but usually a restrained artistic statement. Stained glass raised

little real interest, and secular commissions were practically non-existent, that is, until the stained glass for Coventry Cathedral in 1959 caused such excitement. In particular, John Piper's baptistry window there led to a new attitude to stained glass in England. He had come to stained glass through his painting and theatrical designing, and the drama and architecture in his windows often reflect this. Patrick Reyntiens, who carried Piper's designs into glass, is himself an artist and his own figurative stained glass, in which painting plays an important part, is exceptional. Their long collaboration has included many other commissions, among them the abstract screen for Messrs Sandersons' showrooms in London in 1960, and 12 panels of foliate heads in a Winchester hotel.

With rare exceptions, there has been little secular postwar stained glass of note in England until recently, when those stained-glass artists educated to believe that only the German postwar school was worthy of study stopped imitation and found their own form of expression. Brian Clarke is perhaps the best known of these artists, and his 1978 window for the London headquarters of Thorn Electrical Industries shows an original and refreshing approach, with confidence and ability working with large areas.

'The art of stained glass,' said John Piper, 'is minor when it is mediocre: when it is first class it is major, like any other art.' In France and Germany, postwar stained glass has generally been recognized as a major art: in England and the United States, it had to struggle for recognition.

FAR LEFT This window by Henri Matisse depicts floral patterns in brightly coloured, unpainted glass. The Chapel of the Rosary, Vence, France.

LEFT A window designed by Brian Clarke in 1978 for Thorn House, London.

ABOVE Memorial window by Tim Lewis in All Saints Church, Oystermouth, Wales, 1977.

ABOVE RIGHT Gabriel *Loire's* Symphony Tower of Joy for Children, *or* The Rainbow Tower, *is part of the open-air Museum of Modern Art in Hakone, near Tokyo. The glass tower is made up of some 480 panels of faceted dalle de verre glass, built around a spiral staircase.*

RIGHT Lloyds Insurance Building, London. Architect: Richard Rogers.*

The United States

THE UNITED STATES had no influential figures comparable to Europe's postwar artists and designers, but, rather, new ways were sought of using stained glass in architecture. This experimental approach was often on a huge scale, with one of the biggest commissions being Robert Sowers' 7000-sq-ft (650-sq-m) wall for the American Airlines terminal at Kennedy Airport, executed in the early 1960s in both translucent and opalescent stained glass, and designed to be viewed from outside as well as inside the building. A lively and popular movement in stained glass emerged, initially principally on the West Coast, but then spreading east. The movement's message, simply, was that stained glass was fun. More than anywhere else stained glass in the United States began to appear again in commercial and domestic buildings. The work of Peter Mollica and Ed Carpenter reflects their study of the work of Schaffrath. They were, however, the exception in positively seeking a European influence, since most other stained-glass artists, among them Paul Marioni and Kathie Bunnell, chose to express themselves in a more American tradition, sometimes combining their glass with the use of other materials. Gyoray Kepes' large slab-glass mural for KLM's New York ticket office, for instance, uses aluminium screening and flashing lights to add to its effect.

New Opportunities

EUROPEAN STAINED-GLASS artists, who looked enviously at the scale of stained glass across the Atlantic, were often frustrated by their own countries' attitudes, so they sought commissions elsewhere in the world. In Japan, at Hakone near Tokyo, Gabriel Loire's *dalle de verre* 'Children's Tower' transports its viewers into a magical childhood world of strongly coloured birds, clowns and flowers. The Venezuelan artist Alvio Rodriguez's colossal window in the Corte Suprema de Justica is the work of the Lorin Studios in Chartres. It is, however, the Middle East that has provided an unparalleled opportunity for new stained-glass work: the clear, bright light and the white marble and concrete of its modern architecture provide an ideal setting for the richness of coloured glass. The window walls of the Aramco Mosque at Dahran in Saudi Arabia, by the English artist Alan Younger, are in green, turquoise and pale blue, and include star-shaped panels of sand-blasted calligraphy showing 88 names of God. This work was carried out by Goddard and Gibbs Studios in London, whose great stained-glass domes appear in public buildings and private palaces as well as mosques.

CHAPTER SEVEN

■

LEFT Designed by Gyoray Kepes for the KLM ticket office in New York and composed of slab glass against a perforated aluminium screen, the mural (detail shown) is lit from behind to create the impression of a sparkling night sky and city lights.

Chapter Eight

INTO THE 21st CENTURY

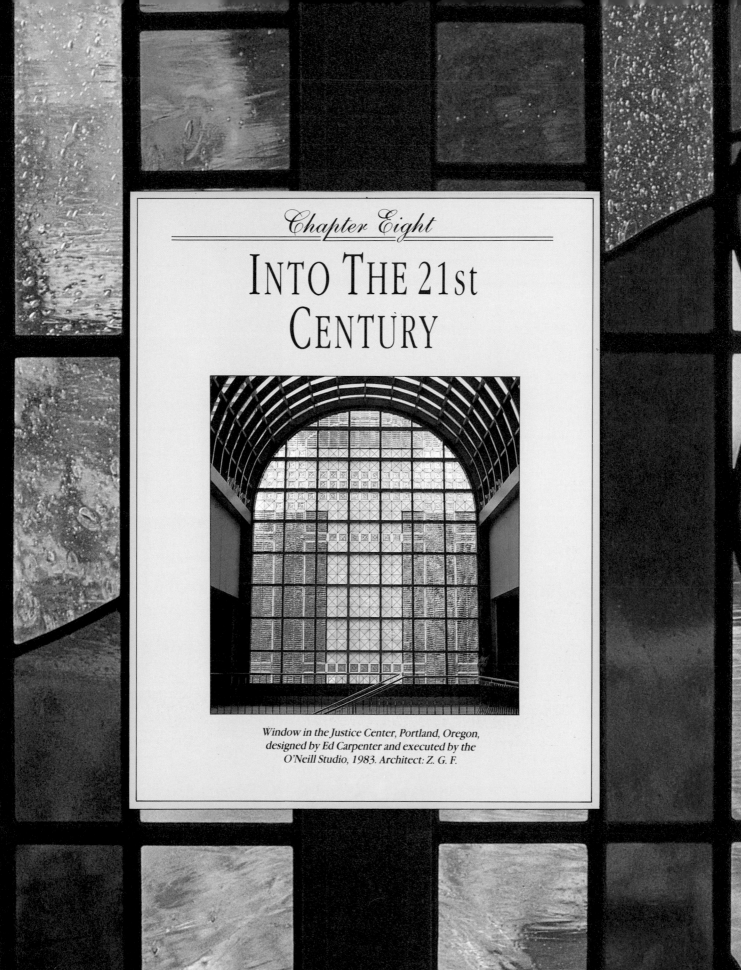

Window in the Justice Center, Portland, Oregon,
designed by Ed Carpenter and executed by the
O'Neill Studio, 1983. Architect: Z. G. F.

OVERLEAF *Detail of a large window (28 sq m), designed by Susan Bradbury for the College of Art & Technology, Newcastle. A muted blue/grey colour scheme was adopted and texture emphasized with a sandblasted band across the entire width of the window.*

STAINED GLASS IS now reaching a popularity that it has not enjoyed since the end of the last century. The architecture of the 1950s and 1960s has largely been condemned by a society tired of the repetitive blandness of the Machine Age, and the purity of functionalism is seen as nothing more than dreariness and mediocrity. Colour and ornament are again returning to building, and in a hundred years the wheel has gone full circle and arts and crafts are again prized for their human value as well as their beauty. This renaissance in decorative arts is now more deeply and widely spread through education – as increasingly books and television communicate the arts – and through the new phenomenon of the practical amateur. This popularity has meant that many art colleges again include stained glass as part of their curriculum, that the craft is more widely practised, albeit by a growing number of individuals rather than a return to larger studios, and that this in turn has generated an exceptional restless talent seeking limited commissions. Another spin-off has been the heightened awareness of the contribution made by stained glass to Western decorative arts. This is apparent from the readiness of museums to now display stained glass, with the new Burrell Collection in Glasgow among the finest, and also a new concern for the care of old glass.

Conservation

RESTORATION IS a term normally applied to the repair and refurbishment of 19th-century and later glass, whereas conservation is more usually concerned with preserving the integrity of older glass, particularly medieval examples. The latter is a science as much as a craft, involving knowledge and training, and it is a highly specialized field of work. The aim of all good conservators is to carry out the minimum work necessary and, where possible, without adding to or taking from the original, and ensuring that any work that is carried out can be reversed at a later date and is fully documented. In the United States, the Corpus Vitrearum, an international body concerned with the preservation of glass, and the Census of Stained Glass in America are two specialist organizations working with national and local preservation groups. In Europe, the Corpus Vitrearum carries out a similar function, by setting voluntary standards and publishing learned articles that both impart knowledge and relay the results of recent research.

One of the largest restoration projects recently undertaken has been at York Minster. Here, early on the morning of 9 July, 1984, a great fire broke out in the north transept extensively damaging the fabric and the

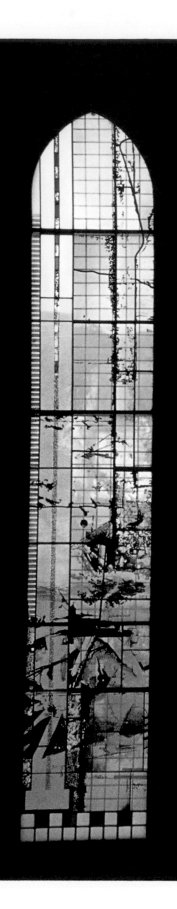

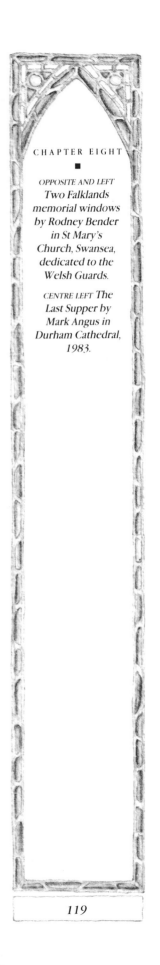

OPPOSITE AND LEFT
**Two Falklands
memorial windows
by Rodney Bender
in St Mary's
Church, Swansea,
dedicated to the
Welsh Guards.**

CENTRE LEFT The
Last Supper by
Mark Angus in
Durham Cathedral,
1983.

RIGHT Chapelle Carmel de Chartres by Jacques Loire.

BELOW RIGHT Detail of the Seven Sacraments window by Amber Hiscott. The Church of our Lady of the Taper, Cardigan, Wales.

BELOW FAR RIGHT Window above the main entrance to St Denis in Vaucresson, France, designed by Jacques Loire and executed in slab glass set in concrete.

16th-century rose window, whose 8,000 separate pieces of glass were badly cracked by the fire. The window had been re-leaded in 1970 and this undoubtedly helped save its destruction. The fire-damaged glass has been carefully removed, cleaned, repaired and replaced in a programme lasting several years. England almost certainly has a greater heritage of 19th-century and earlier stained glass than any other country, and some studios – such as Chapel Studios in Hertfordshire – specialize in the expert care of old glass. Among the few specialist conservation studios the best known is probably that of G King & Son Limited at Norwich.

In the United States, one of the largest projects of recent years was the removal, repair and eventual replacement (in a much changed building) of the 2000-sq-ft (185-sq-m) City of Paris dome in the Neiman-Marcus department store in San Francisco. Restoration was carried out by Cummings Studios, whose careful work included matching replacement glass specially made by the original supplier, the Kokomo Opalescent Company of Indiana. Other major restoration projects have included the impressive 1893–95 skylight in the Breakers, the Newport, Rhode Island, villa built for Cornelius Vanderbilt II, and windows in the late 19th-century courthouse at Hancock County, Ohio.

A New Approach

AN APPRECIATION and study of existing stained glass can be basic to the success of those who use it as a starting point, and a prison for those who are limited to repeating what has gone before. It was the tensions and movement expressed in the work of the modern German artists that enabled them to use a traditional art form in an entirely new way. The stained-glass windows of a Gothic cathedral are frozen pictures locked in time: Schaffrath's work is that of constant motion and controlled activity. The work of this extraordinary man has done more than any other to move stained glass forward and away from its traditional pictorial image. If Europe's contribution to recent stained glass has been an intellectual one, then the American contribution has perhaps been that of irreverence. This ability to see stained glass as an art form, neither bound by the convention of materials or expression, nor limited to the fenestration of a building, has allowed a wonderful new freedom and vitality to characterize recent American work.

LEFT *The glass 'belly' of the Hong Kong Bank. Architect: N Foster.*

STAINED GLASS

∎

RIGHT Stained-glass canopy by Amber Hiscott for Liberty & Co, London.

FAR RIGHT Screen, entitled Treasures of the Mediterranean, designed by Narcissus Quagliata and fabricated by Janet Christensen and Quagliata Mesrahi Studio. The fish, representing Christianity, rises from the corrupt Classical world. The right-hand panel represents the sea.

New Art

IT IS DIFFICULT to recognize the successors to Schaffrath's generation in Germany, although artists such as Karl-Martin Hartmann and Karl Traut are working in their image – but without the opportunities presented by the postwar building boom. The debt to the modern German school of stained glass is immense and international: as in all art, though, just as a new dynamic movement arises in a burst of creative energy, so it will eventually exhaust itself and wither. In France, artists such as Jacques Loire continue the Expressionist pictorial approach of the 1950s and 1960s, while in Italy stained glass – still considered by many to be a sacred art form – awaits popular new acceptance.

There are individuals in Europe who transcend any national label and whose work is international. The Icelandic artist Leifur Breidfjord's stained glass is monochromatic, with strong linear leading and painting. While some think his work is wrong for St Giles' Cathedral in Edinburgh, the city in which he trained, it has been a triumph in his native Reykjavik. The Greek artist Eugenia Polti uses glass as two-dimensional sculpture interpreting space and light in a new way, and her screen for the Trafalgar Hotel in London is a good example of her individual approach.

In Great Britain, lively new talent has arisen, combining the best of a painterly tradition and use of strong colour with a control and lyricism taken from the Continent. Mark Angus's ecclesiastical windows are a fresh and sincere contribution to religious stained glass: his window of the Last Supper in Durham Cathedral is like no other window there, yet it has the monumen-tality of the building's Norman architecture, the majestic dark richness of its surrounding stonework, and a spirituality expressed simply and with moving effect. In the secular field, two among many gifted new artists are Amber Hiscott and Alexander Beleschenko, the latter of whose window at Stockley Park uses colour and pattern in complete harmony with the architecture. In glass decoration, Diane Radford and Lindsey Ball are a successful partnership: their large sandblasted screen in Lime Street Station, Liverpool, is on a scale rarely encountered since John Hutton's great west screen in Coventry Cathedral in 1962. The strength of current British work lies in the depth of talent that exists, much of it generated by the art colleges at Swansea and Wrexham; its weakness is the reluctance of architects to appreciate and use it.

American artistic talent in glass is widespread and diverse, with many individuals working and expressing themselves in new and exciting ways – through Pop Art and Surrealism, mixed mediums and free-standing work. Tom Patti's glass sculptures are a sensitive and very personal use of the inherent qualities of glass itself, neither contrived nor static. David Ruth's stained glass is free of the anchor of formal framing, with bright colours and sometimes with colour replacing lead lines. The work of Ed Carpenter, Narcissus Quagliata, Peter Mollica, Richard Posner and Garth Edwards is very much in the mould of current American stained glass, often using mixed media in a boldly expressive manner that is unfettered by any restraints of convention. In Canada, Ray King shows complete control of scale and material while still being innovative and exciting.

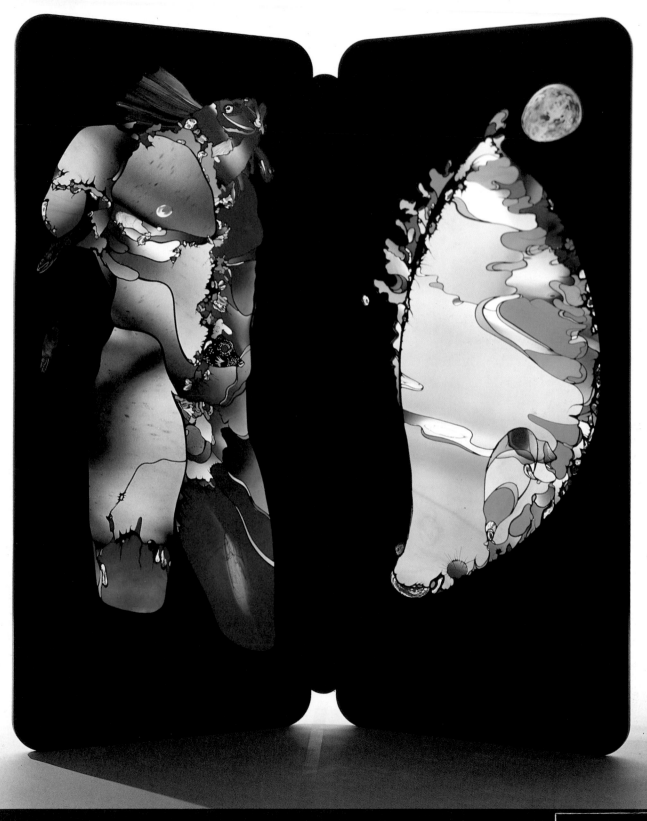

■

RIGHT *Window designed by Ed Carpenter and fabricated by the O'Neill Studio, 1985. Kaiser Permanente Medical Clinic, Portland, Oregon. Architect: B.O.O.R.A.*

BELOW RIGHT *Window, made up of 18 glass-laminate panels, designed by Alexander Beleschenko and fabricated by the Wilhelm Dorix Glass Studio. Stockley Park, Hillingdon, London.*

OPPOSITE TOP LEFT *Porca Miseria, screen designed by Narcissus Quagliata and fabricated by Dorothy Lenehan, depicts a real life 'down and out' living in San Francisco.*

OPPOSITE FAR RIGHT *Window designed by Peter Mollica, 1985. University of Alaska, Fairbanks.*

OPPOSITE LEFT *One of Garth Edwards' popular stained-glass portraits.*

OPPOSITE RIGHT *Glass panel by Peter Mollica, 1984. Private residence, Concord, New Hampshire.*

New Craft

THE SEARCH for new expression in stained glass has led to the new use of old materials, and the introduction of other crafts and technologies. Some new materials have been used for their modern graphic imagery, such as Howard Meehan's incorporation of electronic components in his glass, or Stephen Antonakos's work with neon tube lighting. High technology is also being employed to find new directions for decorative glass; the use of lasers is growing, and the exciting potential of holography has been recognized.

More conventional is the introduction of new colour effects and surface treatments in glass, many of which are now widely available. These include the coating of lead cames with colour or metals, the increasing use of bevelling and mirrors, and the ability to laminate stained glass for both safety and strength, allowing much larger areas to be free of intrusive support. Perhaps with our ability to now transmit the equivalent of 10,000 telephone lines through a single glass fibre no bigger than a human hair, it will soon be possible for natural day lighting of stained glass in a room without windows or skylight. Stained glass is an ongoing and exciting story.

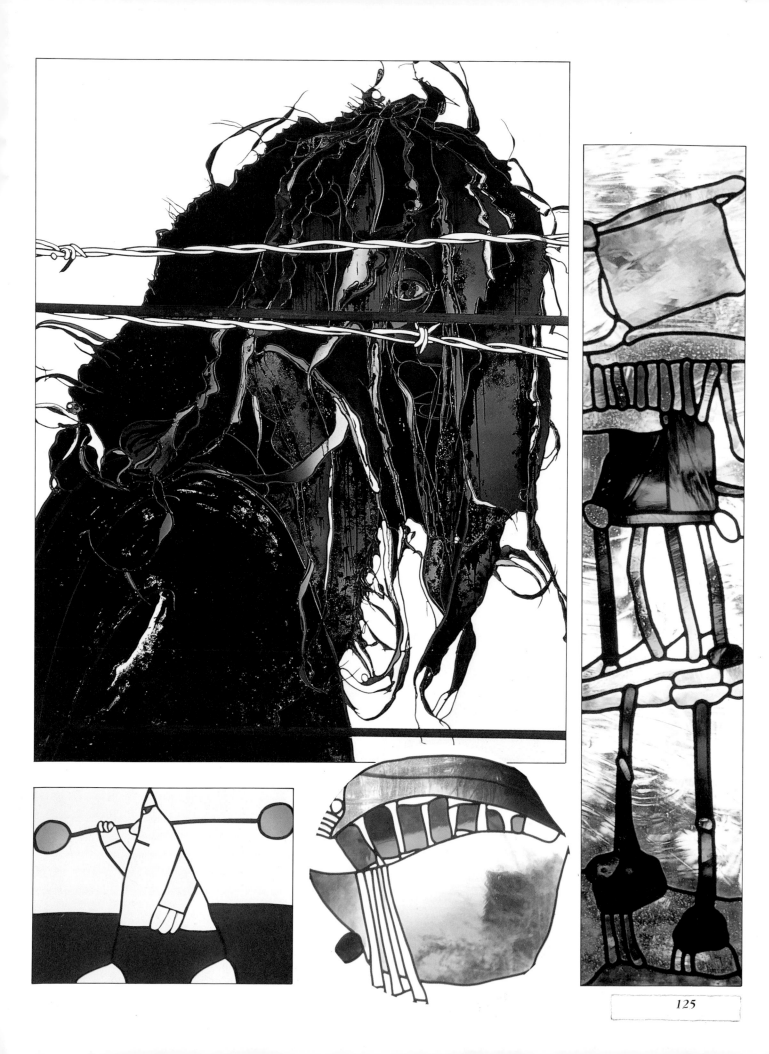

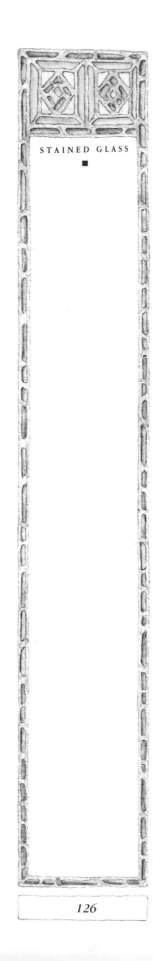

STAINED GLASS

INDEX

Page numbers in *italic* refer to captions and illustrations

A

Aachen Cathedral, 92
Abbot's Hospital, Guildford, 38
abstract design, 64, *72*, 75, 80, 87, 92, 107
acid-etching, 23
aciding, 20
Aesthetic movement, 58–9
air bubbles, 12
Air Force Academy Chapel, New Colorado Springs, 95
Alaska University, *124*
Albers, Josef, 76, 92, 107
Almquist, Carl, 59
amateur work, 16
Angus, Mark, 122
    Last Supper, 119, 122
annealing chambers, 10
ante-types, 30
antique glass, 10, 12, 13, 77
    see also pot-metal glass
Antonakos, Stephen, 124
Aramco Mosque, Dahran, Saudi Arabia, *99*, 115
architecture, 100, 102–3, 118, 122
Arnold, Hugh, 74
Art Deco, 102–3
Art Nouveau, 60, 73–7, 102
art schools, 64, 77, 81, 92, 107, 122
Art Workers' Guild, 64
Arts and Crafts Movement, 64–6, 68, 73
Arundel Cathedral, *15*
Ashdown Park, Sussex, *70*
Ashwin, Frederick, *49*
    Dawning of the Last Day, 49
Atelier d'Art Sacré, 86
Atelier Jacques Simon, *90*
Augsburg Cathedral, 26
Austria, 23, 75

B

Ball, Lindsey, 122
Balmoral Castle, Pimlico, London, 106
Basilika of St Gereon, Cologne, *95, 110*
Bath Abbey, 50
Bauhaus School, 92, 107
Bazaine, Jean, 86
Beleschenko, Alexander, 122, *124*
Belgium, 36, 39, 43, 77, 81
Bender, Rodney, *119*
Betton and Evans, 46
bevelling, 107
Bing, Samuel, 68, 73, 77
Bissiers, Roger, 87
blown glass *see* glass blowing
Bodley, GF, 50, 52
Bolae studio, 107
Bolton, William Jay, 61
Bonnard, Pierre, 73
Bony, Paul, *84*, 112
Bradbury, Susan, 118
Bradford Cathedral, *54*
Braque, Georges, *85, 87*, 112
Breakers, Newport, Rhode Island, 120
brilliant cutting, 23
Breidfjord, Leifur, 122

Britten and Gilson, 65, 66
Brown, Ford Maddox, 55
    Adam and Noah, 56
Buchanan Street Tea Rooms, Glasgow, 75
Bunnell, Kathie, 115
Burlison and Grylls, 49
Burne-Jones, Edward, *49*, 55, 58, 77
    Angel and Musician, 58
    Baptism of Christ, 57
    Flight into Egypt, 41, 56
    Kingdom of Heaven, 55
    Vyner Memorial window, 55
Buschulte, Wilhelm, *110–11*, 111
Buss, Arthur, *95, 97*

C

Café Royal Oyster Bar, Edinburgh, *72*
Cakebread, Robey and Co, 107
calms, 22
Cambridge Camden Society, 48
Cambridge University, 38, *79*, 95, 96
    see also King College Chapel
Camperdonk, Heinrich, 92, 107
cames, *22*
canopies, 30
Canterbury Cathedral, *22, 26*, 29, 30-1, *34*
Carpenter, Ed, 115, *117*, 122, *124*
Carre, Jean, 9
Carson, Pine and Scott, 102
cartoons, *17–18*, 18, 55, 94
cathedral glass, 13
cementing *see* sealing
Census of Stained Glass, 118
Century Guild, 64
Chagall, Marc, 87, 90–1, *90–1*, 112
Chance, William Edward, 46
Chance Brothers, 13, 46
Chapel of the Rosary, Vence, *113*
Chapel Studios, 120
Chareau, Pierre, 103
Chartres Cathedral, 26, *26–7*, 31, *33, 38–9*, 61, 83, 84, *120*
Child, Alfred, 66, 81
Christ Church Cathedral, Oxford, 55
churches, 48, 74–5, 76, 80, 86, 95, 112–3
    Acomb, N Yorks, 38
    All Saints, Boyne Hill, Berks, *46*
    All Saints, Middleton Cheney, Northants, 56
    All Saints, Oystermouth, *113*
    All Saints, Tudeley, Kent, *90*, 91
    All Saints, West Bromwich, Staffs, 59
    Bottrop, Germany, *107*, 110–11
    Castlehaugh, Co Cork, 81
    Christ Episcopal, Bronx, NY, 60
    Christ Episcopal, Rye, NY, 73
    Christ Kerk, Dinslaken, 92
    Christchurch, Southgate, London, 56
    Church of the Incarnation, NY, 50
    Creech, Wakeham, Dorset, *47*
    Evreux, France, *36*
    First Presbyterian, Stamford, Conn, 95, 97

    Fyvie Kirk, Scotland, 73
    Great Barton, Suffolk, *49*
    Holy Trinity, Meole Brace, Shrops, *42*
    Holy Trinity, Sloane Street, London, 58
    Lamarsh, Essex, *63, 66*
    Lydiard Tregoze, Wilts, *37*, 38
    Manningham, Bradford, *54*
    Nettlestead, Kent, 52
    Newport, Co Mayo, 81
    Northchapel, Sussex, *67*
    Notre Dame, Douai, 111
    Notre-Dame-de-Raincy, *84*
    Notre-Dame-de-Toute-Grace, Assy, *84*, 86–7, 90
    Our Lady of the Taper, Cardigan, *120*
    Pelham Bay, NY, 61
    Riverside, Manhattan, NY, 84
    Sacred Heart, Audincourt, 83
    St Andrew's, Trent, Dorset, *44*
    St Ann and the Holy Trinity, NY, 61
    St Barnabas', Hengoed, Shrops, *49*
    St Cuthbert's, Edinburgh, *72*
    St Denis, Vaucresson, *120*
    St Dominique's, Varangeville, *87*
    St Dunstan's, Cheam, Surrey, *42*
    St Engelbert, Solingen, 92
    St George's, W Grinstead, Sussex, *52*
    St Jacob, Reuthe/Vorarlberg, 92
    St John the Evangelist, High Cross, Herts, *53*
    St John the Baptist, Cookham Dean, Berks, *49*
    St Maria-im Kapital, Germany, 92
    St Marks, Stapleford, Sussex, *53*
    St Martin, Brampton, Cumberland, 58
    St Mary Magdalen, Paddington, London, 59
    St Mary Mother of Jesus, Brooklyn, NY, 95
    St Mary the Virgin, Hanley Castle, Worcs, 50, *51*
    St Mary's, Derby, 43
    St Mary's, Fairford, Glos, 38, *38, 52*
    St Mary's, Kelvedon, Essex, *64*
    St Mary's, Köln Kalk, *109*
    St Mary's, Slough, Bucks, *66, 72, 75*, 94
    St Mary's, Stamford, Lincs, 65
    St Mary's, Swansea, *119*
    St Matthew's, Ipswich, Suffolk, 71
    St Maximin, Metz, *88*
    St Michael and All Angels, Gt Witley, Worcs, *38*, 39
    St Michael and All Angels, Lyndhurst, Hants, 55
    St Michael's, Aylsham, Norfolk, *61*
    St Michael's, Brighton, Sussex, *41, 56–7*
    St Peter and St Paul, Cattistock, Dorset, 58
    St Peter's, Aachen, *111*
    St Vincent Ferrer, NY, 84
    Three Kings, Neuss, *80*
    Trinity, Manhattan, NY, 60
    Wickhambreaux, Kent, 77
Clarke, Brian, 113, *113*
Clarke, Geoffrey, *93*, 94
Clarke, Harry, 66, 81

    Adoration of the Magi, 70
    Last Judgement . . ., 81
    The Nativity, 81
Clayton and Bell, 49–50, *51*, 52, 83
clear glass, 9, 12, 13, 29
Clutterbuck, Charles, *61*
Cocteau, Jean, *88*
Colearne House, Auchterarder, Scotland, *72*
Colman, Samuel, 68
colours, 9, 10, 12–13, 20–1, 46, 52, 64–5
    monochrome, 92, 111, 122
    tone, 20, 65
Comper, Ninian, 52, 74
Connick, Charles J, 83–4
conservation, 39, 86, 118, 120
copperfoil framing, 22
Corning Museum of Glass, 73
Corpus Vitrearum, 118
Cottars Howff, Edinburgh, *100*
Cottier, Daniel, 59
Couturier, *Father* Marie-Alain, 86–7
Coventry Cathedral, *93*, 94, 113, 122
Cram, Ralph Adams, 82–3, 84
crown glass, 12
Crystal Palace, 74, 103
Cummings Studio, 120
cutlines, *18*, 18
cutting, 20
cylinders *see* muffs

D

Daily Express building, 103
dalle de verre see slab glass
Dana-Thomas house, Springfield, Ill., 76
Davis, Lewis, 64, *64*
    The Annunciation, 64
Derix Glass Studio, 111
design, *16–18*, 17, 55, 80, 94
    abstract, 64, *72*, 75, 80, 87, 92, 107
    ready-made, 35
destruction, 37, 38, 39, 86, 94, 110, 118, 120
Desvallières, Georges, 86
distortion, 22
Diversarum Artium Schedula, 9
domestic buildings, 58, 64, 70, 74, 75, 76, 100, *106*, 120, *124*
Dorchester Abbey, 31
drawing, 13
Drury, Alfred, 66
Durham Cathedral, *119*, 122
Duycking, Everett, 38

E

Easton, Hugh, 74, 94
Edwards, Garth, 122
    The Weightlifter, 124
Ely, Henry, 60
Ely Cathedral, 37
embossing, 23, 106
    French, 106
enamel painting, 21, 35–6, 37–9
England *see* Great Britain
engraving, 23, 106
Eton College Chapel, 81, *81*

F

faïence, 8
Faulkner, Charles, 55

Favrile glass, 61
firing, 9, 21, 81
flashing, 12, 33,
flat glass, 13, 106
float-glass, 13
fluxes, 9
Foster Associates, 103
framing, 22–3
    copperfoil, 22
    leading, 22, *22*, 64, 65, 111, 112
France, 12, 18, 33–4, 39, 68, 75, 77, 80, 86–7, 90–1, 112, 122
French embossing, 106
functionalism, 74, 76, 77
fusing, 13, 21

G

Galerie d'Orléans, 103
Gallé, Emile, 77
Gaudí, Antonio, 77
Geddes, Wilhelmina, 66, *67*, 81
    Te Deum window, 81
Germany, 18, 33, 36, 60, 75–6, 80, 92–3, 103, 107, 110–11, 122
Walter Gibbs and Sons, 49, 106
glass:
    antique, 10, 12, 13, 77
    bevelled, 107
    constituents, 9
    embossed, 23, 106
    engraved, 23, 106
    flat, 13, 106
    float, 13
    'grisaille', *28*, 29, 30, 83
    history, 8–10
    medieval, 9, 12, 20, 22, *22*, 37
    mirror, 106
    monochrome, 92, 111, 122
    opalescent, 12, 60–1, 68, 76–7, 77, 115, 120
    plate, 13
    pot-metal, 12, 37, 46, 77, 80, 83
    Roman, 8, 9, 10, 12
    slab 13, 65, *83*, 94–5, *96*, *114*, *120*
    types of, 8, 9–10, 12–13, 37, 46
    white, 10, 12, 65, 75, 77
glass blowing, *7*, *8–13*, 10, 12, 65
    see also production methods
The Glass House, 66
Gloag, Isabel, 66, *66*
Gloucester Cathedral, 52
Goddard and Gibbs Studios, *15*, *97*, *99*, 106, 115
Goodhue, Wright, 84
Gothic Revival, 43, 48
Gothic style, 26–35, 82–4
    see also medieval glass
Great Britain, 9, 18, 23, 29, 33, 35–7, 73, 80, 82–3, 94–5, 103, 112–3, 122
    Ireland, 66, 80–1
    Scotland, 75
'grisaille', *28*, 29, 30, 83
Gruber, Francis, 87
Gruber, Jacques, 77
guilds, 64
Guthrie, Gordon, 75, 83
Guthrie, J and W, 75, 83
Gwilt, C Edwin, *50*
Gyles, Henry, 38

H

Hadassah Medical Centre, Jerusalem, 91
Hagen Railway Station, W Germany, *103*
Hampton Court, Mddx, 46

handmade glass *see* glass blowing
John Hardman and Co, *42*, 43, 83
Hartmann, Karl-Martin, 122
Haworth Art Gallery, Accrington, Lancs, *68*, 73
Healy, Michael, 66, 81
Heaton Butler and Bayne, 49, *49*, 50, *100*
Hebert-Stevens, Jean, 86
Hedgeland, George, *71*
Heide Glasshouse, 61
heraldic devices, 30, 31, 33, 38, 46, *100*
Hereford Cathedral, 29
Hiscott, Amber, *120*, 122, *122*
history:
    Aesthetic movement, 58–9
    Art Deco, 102–3
    Art Nouveau, 60, 73–7, 102
    Arts and Crafts Movement, 64–6, 68, 73
    glass, 8–10
    Gothic revival, 43, 48
    Gothic style, 26–35, 82–4
    medieval period, 9, 12, 20, 22, 37
    modern period, 80–124
    Opus Francigenum, 33
    Pre-Raphaelites, 54–5
    Reformation, 36–7
    Renaissance style, 35–6, 37
    Romanesque style, 33, 34
    Scientific Romantics, 60
    stained glass, 25–77
    Victorian period, 42–61
Holiday, Henry, 49, 59, *59*
Holland, 9, 23
holography, 124
Hone, Evie, 66, 81, *81*
    Crucifixion and Last Supper, 81
    St Cecilia, 69
Hong Kong Bank, *121*
Horta, Victor, 77
Houses of Parliament, London, 43
Howard, Frank, *71*
Hunt, William Holman, 54
Hutton, John, 122

I

iconography, 31, 80
Image, Selwyn, 64, *70*
images, 29–31
industrial revolution, 42
inter-war period, 80, 107
Ireland, 66, 80–1
    see also Great Britain
Italy, 23, 33, 60

J

Jerningham, William, 39
Jesse trees, *26*, 31, *33*
Johannesbund Chapel, Leutesdorf, 92, *92*, 111
Peter Jones, 103
Judson Studios, 95
Justice Center, Portland, Oregon, *117*

K

Kaiser Permanente Medical Clinic, Portland, Oregon, *124*
Kempe, Charles Eamer, 52, *52–3*, 55, 64, *71*, 74
    Expulsion of Adam and Eve, 52
Kennedy Airport, 115
kilns, 21

G King and Son, 120
King, Ray, 122
Kings College Chapel, Cambridge, 30, 37, *37*, 50
Klee, Paul, 92
KLM building, NY, 115
Klos, Joachim, 111
Kokomo Opalescent Company, 120

L

La Farge, John, 59, 61, 68, 83
    The Annunciation, 77, *77*
Lamb, Joseph and Richard, 61
Lancing College Chapel, Sussex, 95, *97*
Lanercost Priory, Cumbria, *69*
lasers, 124
Lavers Barraud and Westlake, 49, *49*, 50, *59*,
Lawson, John, *15*
leaded lights, 95
leading, *22*, 22, 64, 65, 111, 112
Lee, Lawrence, *93*, 94
Léger, Fernand, *83*, 86, 112
lehrs, 10, *12–13*
Lenehan, Dorothy, *124*
Lever House, NY, 103, *106*
Lewis, Tim, *113*
Liberty and Co, 73, *122*
Lime Street Station, Liverpool, 122
Linden Glass Company, Chicago, 76
line work, 21
van Linge, Abraham and Bernard, 37, 38, 39
Liverpool Catholic Cathedral, 94–5, 95
Lloyds Insurance Building, 103, *114*
Loire, Gabriel, 95, *97*, *114*, 115
Loire, Jacques, *120*, 122
London Glaziers' Guild, 38
Lord Nelson, Old Kent Road, London, 106
Lorin, Nicholas, 60
Lorin Studios, 115
Lowndes, Mary, *63*, 66, *66*

M

Mackintosh, Charles Rennie, *74*, 75
Mackmurdo, AH, 64
Maeght Museum, France, *85*
Maison de Verre, Paris, 103
Marcq, Charles and Brigitte, *90*, 91, 112
Marioni, Paul, 115
Marshall, PP, 55
Martyn, Edward, 81
Matisse, Henri, *112*, *113*
matting, 20, *20*, 65
medieval glass, 9, 12, 20, 22, *22*, 37
    see also Gothic style
Meehan, Howard, 124
Meistermann, Georg, 92, *95*, *102*, *107*, *109–10*, 110–11
merchants' marks, 35
Metropolitan Museum of Art, NY, 73
Metz Cathedral, 91
Millais, John Everett, 54
mirror glass, 106
modern period, 80–124
Mollica, Peter, 115, 122, *124*
monochromes, 92, 111, 122
Morris, William, 54–5, 58, 64
Morris and Co, *41*, *42*, 54, *56–8*, 77
Charles Hosmer Morse Foundation, Florida, 73

moulding, 10, 12, 13, 65
muffs, 10, *10*, *12*
Museum of Modern Art, Hakone, Tokyo, *114*, 115
Museum of Modern Art, NY, 73

N

Nabis, the, 68, 73
National Cathedral, Washington, DC, 52
Nazarenes, 60
Neiman-Marcus building, 120
New, Keith, *93*, 94, 95
New College Chapel, Oxford, 39
Newcastle College of Art and Technology, *118*
Nicholson, AK, 94
Niton House, Isle of Wight, *50*
Notre Dame, Paris, 34

O

O'Connor, Michael, *44*, 46
O'Neill Studio, *117*
opalescent glass, 12, 60–1, 68, 76–7, 77, 115, 120
Opus Francigenum, 33
Oudinot, Eugène Stanislas, 60
    Supper at Emmaus, 60
Oundle School Chapel, Northants, 94, 95
Oussuaire de Douaumont, Verdun, 86
Oxford University, 38, 39, 59

P

painting, 20–1, 33, 35, 37, 42, 60, 65, 80, 112
    enamel, 21, 35–6, 37–9
Parsons, Karl, 74
patterns *see* cutlines
Patti, Tom, 122
Paxton, Joseph, 74, 103
Payne, Henry, 74
Perret, August, *84*
Peterhouse College, Cambridge 38
Piper, John, *79*, 94–5, *95–6*, 113
plate glass, 13
Poensgen, Jochem, 92, 111
polishing, 13
Polti, Eugenia, 122
Posner, Richard, 122
post-war period, 92, 94–5, 100–24
pot-metal glass, 12, 37, 46, 77, 80, 83
    see also antique glass
Powell, JH, *42*
Powell, James, 46, 49, *49*, 59, 83
    Christ in Glory, 83
Pre-Raphaelite Movement, 54–5
pressure, 22
Price, William and Joshua, *38*, 39
Prikker, Jan Thorn, 80, *80*, 92, *103*, 107
    Orange, 92
Prior's Early English glass, 13, 65
production methods, 8, 9, 10, 13
    blowing, *7*, *8–13*, 10, 12, 65
    stained glass, 16–23, *16–23*
    tools, *13*, 18, *18*, 20, 106
Protestant reformation, 36-7
Prudde, John, 35
public buildings, 38–9, 59, 76–7, 79, 91, *91*, 95, *96*, 100–24, *100*, *102–3*, *108*, *113–15*, *117*, *121–2*, *124*
public houses, *100*, *104*, 106, 107
Pugin, Augustus, *42*, 43, *43*, 46
puntys, 12
Purser, Sarah, 66, 81

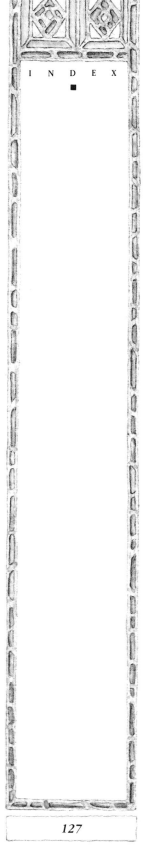

STAINED GLASS
■

Q

Quagliata, Narcissus, 122
  Porca Miseria, *124*
  *Treasures of the
  Mediterranean*, *122*
Queen's Head, Crouch End,
  London, *104*

R

Radford, Diane, 122
Rambusch Studio, 103
reamy glass, 12
Red Cross building, Washington,
  DC, *68*
Reims Cathedral, 34, *34*
Renaissance style, 35–6, 37
repair *see* conservation
restoration *see* conservation
Reyntiens, Patrick, 94, *95–6*, 113
Robinson College, Cambridge,
  79, 95, *96*
Rochdale Town Hall, Lancs, *100*,
  102
Rodriguez, Alvio, 115
Rogers, Richard, 103, *114*
rolling, 13
Roman glass, 8, 9, 10, 12
Romanesque style, 33, 34
rose windows, *27*, 29, 34, *34*, 39,
  49, *96–7*, 120
Rosenkranz, Arild
  The Annunciation, 77
Rossetti, Dante Gabriel, 54, *54*,
  55, *64*
Rouault, Georges, 80, *84*, 86
Roussel, Ker-Xavier, 73
Royal Bavarian Glass Painting
  Studio, 60
Ruskin, John, 54, 64
Ruth, David, 122

S

Sainsbury Art Centre, Norwich,
  103
St Antonius Hospital Chapel,
  Eschweiler, 108
St Denis Abbey, 26, 31, *32*, 33
St Giles' Cathedral, Edinburgh,
  122
St John the Divine Cathedral, NY,
  82–3, 84
St Martin's Cathedral, Ypres, 81

St Mary's College Chapel, Oscott,
  Warwicks, *42–3*
St Peter and St Paul Cathedral,
  Washington, DC, 82
The Salisbury, Harringay,
  London, 107
Salisbury Cathedral, 38
sand, 8, 9
sandblasting, 23, 107
sanguine, 35
Schaffrath, Ludwig, 92, *108*, 111,
  115, 122
Schreiter, Johannes, 92, *92*, 111
Scientific Romantics, 60
Scotland, 75
  see also Great Britain
Scott, Gilbert, 50
sculptures, 122
sealing, 22, *22*
seedy glass, 12
Sens Cathedral, 34, *34*
shading *see* matting
Shaw, Richard Norman, 64
Shrigley and Hunt, 59
silver staining, 52, *53*
silvering, 106
slab glass, 13, 65, *83*, 94–5, *96*,
  114, *120*
Slater, Francisco, *38*
soldering, 22
Sommerfeld House, Berlin, 107
Southwark Cathedral, 94
Sowers, Robert, 115
Spain, 33, 77
Spence, *Sir* Basil, 94
spun glass *see* crown glass
stabilizers, 9
stained glass, 10, 16, 20
  abstract design, 64, 72, 75, 80,
    87, 92, 107
  cartoons, *17–18*, 18, 55, 94
  design, *16–18*, 17, 35, 55, 80,
    94
  destruction, 37, 38, 39, 86, 94,
    110, 118, 120
  history, 25–77
  installation, 22–3
  modern, 80–124
  price of, 30
  production, 16–23, *16–23*
staining, 21, 33
statues, 30
Stewart, William, 72
Stock Exchange, Chicago, 102
Stockley Park, 122, *124*
Strawberry Hill, 43
streaky cathedral glass, 13
Street, G E, 50
striations, 12

studios, 43, 48–50, 52, 54–5, 60,
  65–6, 75, 86, 95, 103, 107,
  111, 115, 120
Sullivan, Louis, 102
surface decoration, 23
Sutton, Baptista, 38
symbolism *see* iconography

T

taxation, 9, 106, 110
texture, 13
Thomas, Brian, 95
Thorn Electrical Industries
  building, 113, *113*
Tiffany, Louis Comfort, 22, 59,
  60, 61, 68, *68*, 73, 75–6, 102
  Boer War window, *72*
  Four Seasons, 68
  Reading of the Scrolls, *60*
  St Michael, 73
tone, 20, 65
tools, *13*, 18, *18*, 20, 106
The Tottenham, Oxford Street,
  London, 106
Tower, Walter Ernest, 52
Trafalgar Hotel, London, 122
Traherne, Margaret, 95
Traut, K, 122
Travers, Martin, 94
An Túr Gloine, 66, 81
Twelve Labours of the Months,
  25, 35
types, 30

U

United Nations, NY, 91, *91*
United States, 12–13, 18, 23, 38,
  50, 52, 59–61, 64, 76, 80–4,
  95, 102–3, 107, 115, 120–2
  see also Tiffany
University College, Oxford, 38
Upjohn, Richard, 60–1

V

Van Der Rohe, Mies, 103, *106*
Van Doesburg, Theo, 92, 107
van de Velde, Henry, 77
Victoria and Albert Museum,
  London, *50*, *64*
Victorian period, *41–7*, *42–61*,
  49–61

Viollet-le-Duc, Eugène-Emanuel,
  60
Vitrearius, Laurence, 9
Vuillard, Edouard, 73

W

Wailes, William, 46
  Flight into Egypt, *46*
Walpole, Horace, 39, 43
Waltham Abbey, Essex, *49*
Ward and Hughes, 50
Warrington, William, *42*, *43*, 46
water glass, 13
Webb, Christopher and Geoffrey,
  74, 94
Webb, Philip, 55
Wendling, Anton, 92, 107
West German Radio Station,
  Cologne, *102*, 110–11
Westlake, NHJ, *49*
Westminster Abbey, 39, 50
Whall, Christopher, *65*, 66, 74,
  75, 81
  Virgin and Child . . ., *65*
white glass, 10, 12, 65, 75, 77
White House, Washington, DC,
  68, 102
Whitefriars Glass Works, 46
Willement, Thomas, *44*, 46, *47*
Willet, William, 83–4
William of Sens, 29
Willow Tea Room, Glasgow, *74*
Wilson, Tom
  Tennis Player, *72*
Winchester Cathedral, 52
Winchester College, *44*, 46
window glass, 9, 12, 13
Winston, Charles, 46
Wolmark, Alfred, *72*, 75, 94
Wooldridge, Harry Ellis, 59
Worcester College, Oxford, *59*
Wright, Frank Lloyd, 76, 102
Wyatt, James, 39

Y

York Minster, *26*, *28–9*, 29, 33,
  38, 83, 118, 120
Young, Henry Wynd, 75, 83
Younger, Alan, *99*, 115

Individual churches mentioned in the text are all
indexed under the general term: churches, followed by
their names and locations. All other ecclesiastical
buildings are entered under their individual names
only, e.g. Canterbury Cathedral.